Christian Lindtner

Revelation of Bodhicittam

Nāgārjuna's Bodhicittavivaraṇam

Angkor Verlag

Revelation of Bodhicittam. Nāgārjuna's Bodhicittavivaraṇam./Lindtner, Christian. – Frankfurt, Angkor Verlag 2015.

© Dr. Christian Lindtner

Editing: Niels Jørgen Lindtner, Guido Keller

Special thanks to the friendly staff of Dharma Publishing!

Coverimages: Gandharan Athena, Musée national des arts asiatiques, Guimet, Paris. Photo von Uploadmo (Wikipedia) [front]
Zeus on the throne, snippet of coin [back]

Printed by Books on Demand GmbH, Norderstedt

ISBN: 978-3-943839-32-6
E-Book: 978-3-943839-33-3

Table of Contents

Introduction

This regrettably neglected text comprises 112 stanzas (anuṣṭubh) introduced by a brief prologue in prose. It has sometimes been grouped as a tantric work, but a glance at its contents shows how unwarranted such a classification is.

The Bodhicittavivaraṇa is never mentioned or cited by Buddhapālita or Candrakīrti. On the other hand it forms one of the basic authorities for Bhavya in his most mature work, the Ratnapradīpa. It is never quoted in his earlier works, the Tarkajvālā, Prajñāpradīpa, and [*Kara-]talaratna. Among other 'good' authors citing the Bodhicittavivaraṇa are especially Asvabhāva and Śāntarakṣita. I have also come across scores of quotations by other commentators; fortunately several of these are in Sanskrit. It is my general impression that the Yuktiṣaṣṭikā, Catuḥstava, and Bodhicittavivaraṇa are the most frequently quoted among all works ascribed to Nāgārjuna in later Indian literature.

The style of the Bodhicittavivaraṇa is similar to that of the Yuktiṣaṣṭikā, Ratnāvalī, and Catuḥstava. From a historical point of view the most significant feature of this text is its extensive critique of Vijñānavāda; i.e. Buddhist idealism testified in the Laṅkāvatārasūtra. Having seen how vehemently Nāgārjuna attacks any kind of acceptance of svabhāva, one would also expect him to have criticized those who might have thought themselves justified in maintaining the absolute existence of vijñāna, or citta. But in the texts dealt with hitherto this happens only incidentally. The Bodhicittavivaraṇa provides us with the missing link.

None of Nāgārjuna's other works exhibit such a well-balanced and coherent structure as the Bodhicittavivaraṇa. This is to some extent a natural consequence of the fact that the theme is at once simple and comprehensive: bodhicitta. It has a relative aspect consisting in the desire (prārthanā) for the bodhi of all living beings, and an absolute consisting in the unlimited cognition of śūnyatā, or bodhi. The Bodhicittavivaraṇa thus provides us with a compendium of the practice and theory of Mahāyāna addressed to Bodhisattvas, gṛhasthas as well as pravrajitas. It may indeed be said to be nothing but a vivaraṇa of the celebrated formula of RĀ IV, 96: śūnyatākaruṇāgarbham ekeṣāṃ bodhisādhanam.

Sanskrit fragments apart, only two Tibetan versions of the Bodhicittavivaraṇa are at our disposal. I have identified these in the section on sources and variants in Part I, using the abbreviations A, B, and C. B, as we would expect from the names of the revisors, is an excellent piece of work, and it forms the basis of my edition. Throughout I have carefully compared A and C. In a few cases A has proved invaluable, for example for verse 16, left out in B due to haplography (homoearcton). C is a commentary of high standard. It quotes pratīkas from all the 112 stanzas and explains all debatable points exhaustively. In a few cases, like A, it permits us to emend corruptions in B. I have, however, only registered variants in A and C when they affect the sense in such a way that it may possibly be more authentic than the one transmitted by B.

I present here a synopsis of the text, followed by notes on the individual verses.

Synopsis

Prologue

The theme of this treatise is bodhicitta. Saṁvṛtitaḥ [from a relative perspective] it is a yearning for the bodhi of all living beings; paramārthataḥ [from the absolute perspective] it is the realization of śūnyatā; i.e., bodhi.

Content

The significance of developing bodhicitta. (1-3)

Refutation of the belief in an ātman, a permanent soul and a creator, as held by tīrthikas. (4-9)

Refutation of the existence of the skandhas, as held by the Śrāvakas. (10-25)

Refutation of the fundamentals of the Vijñānavāda: trisvabhāva, svasaṁvedanā, āśrayaparivṛtti, and ālayavijñāna. In reality, vijñāna is dependent, momentary, illusory, and empty. (26-56)

All internal and external dharmas are pratītyasamutpanna, or śūnya. To understand this is to realize the absolute bodhicitta, or liberation from the bonds of karma due to the kleśas. (57-72)

A Bodhisattva who has thus become a Buddha is motivated by karuṇā (that is, by the power of his previous praṇidhānas) to apply all possible means (= upāyakauśalya) in order to rescue all beings from samsāra. (73-104)

Conclusion

The reader is encouraged to produce bodhicitta. (105-111)

A final dedication of merit. (112)

Bodhicittavivaraṇa

| dngos po thams cad dang bral ba | | phung po khams dang skye mched kyi | | gzung dang 'dzin pa rnam spangs pa | | chos bdag med pas mnyam nyid pas | | rang sems gdod nas ma skyes pa | | stong pa nyid kyi rang bzhin no | | zhes bya ba 'byung ngo | | sangs rgyas bcom ldan 'das rnams dang | byang chub sems dpa' chen po de rnams kyis ji ltar byang chub chen por thugs bskyed pa de bzhin du | bdag gis kyang sems can ma bsgral ba rnams bsgral ba dang | ma grol ba rnams grol ba dang | dbugs ma byung ba rnams dbugs dbyung ba dang | yongs su mya ngan las ma 'das pa rnams yongs su mya ngan las bzla ba'i phyir dus 'di nas bzung nas byang chub snying po la mchis kyi bar du byang chub chen por sems bskyed par bgyi'o | | byang chub sems dpa' gsang sngags kyi sgor spyad pa spyod pa rnams kyis de ltar kun rdzob kyi rnam pas byang chub kyi sems smon pa'i rang bzhin can bskyed nas | don dam pa'i byang chub kyi sems bsgom pa'i stobs kyis bskyed par bya ba yin pas de'i phyir de'i rang bzhin bshad par bya'o ||

1

| byang chub sems kyi bdag nyid dngos |
| dpal ldan rdo rje rnams btud de |
| byang chub sems kyi bsgom pa ni |
| srid pa 'jig de bdag gis bshad |

2

| sangs rgyas rnams kyi byang chub sems |
| bdag dang phung sogs rnam rig gi |
| rtog pa rnams kyis ma bsgribs pa |
| rtag tu stong nyid mtshan nyid bzhed |

It has been stated: "Due to the sameness [or] selflessness of phenomena, one's own mind – devoid of all entities, exempt from the skandhas, elements, sense-fields, and subject and object – is originally unborn; in essence empty."

Just as the Buddhas, our Lords, and the great Bodhisattvas have produced the thought of Great Enlightenment (mahā-bodhicitta), thus I shall also, from now until [we all dwell] in the heart of enlightenment, produce the thought of Great Enlightenment in order to save living beings unsaved, liberate those not liberated, console those not consoled, and lead to nirvana those who have not arrived at nirvana.

When a Bodhisattva, having practiced a course by way of mantras, has thus produced the bodhicitta that in its relative aspect has the nature of aspiration, he must by means of meditational development produce the absolute bodhicitta. Therefore I will reveal its nature.

1

Bowing to the glorious Vajrasattvas embodying the mind of enlightenment, I shall expound the development of the bodhicitta that abolishes [the three kinds of] existence [in saṃsāra].

2

The Buddhas maintain that bodhicitta is not enveloped in notions conscious of a self, skandhas, and so forth, [but] is always marked by being empty [of any such notions].

3

| snying rjes brlan pa'i sems kyis ni |
| 'bad pas bsgom par bya ba yin |
| thugs rje'i bdag nyid sangs rgyas kyis |
| byang chub sems 'di rtag tu bsgoms |

4

| mu stegs can gyis gang brtags pa |
| bdag de rigs pas rnam dpyad na |
| phung rnams kun gyi nang rnams na |
| gang zhig gnas kyang rnyed ma yin |

5

| phung rnams yod kyi de rtag min |
| de yang bdag gi ngo bo min |
| gang yang rtag dang mi rtag gnyis |
| rten dang brten pa'i dngos po med |

6

| bdag ces bya ste yod min na |
| byed po zhes bya ga la rtag |
| chos can yod na chos rnams la |
| 'jig rten na ni spyod pa 'jug |

7

| gang phyir rtag pas don byed pa |
| rim dang cig car gyis min pa |
| de phyir phyi rol nang du ni |
| rtag pa'i dngos de med pa nyid |

8

| gal te nus na ci de ltos |
| de ni cig car dngos 'byin 'gyur |
| gang zhig dngos gzhan la ltos la |
| de ni rtag dang nus ldan min |

3

[Those] with minds [only] tinged by compassion must develop [bodhicitta] with particular effort. This bodhicitta is constantly developed by the compassionate Buddhas.

4

When the self imagined by the tīrthikas is analyzed logically, it obtains no place within the [five] skandhas.

5

If it were [identical with] the skandhas [the self] would not be permanent, but the self has no such nature. And between things permanent and impermanent a container-content relationship is not [possible].

6

When there is no so-called self how can the so-called creator be permanent? [Only] if there were a subject might one begin investigating its attributes in the world.

7

Since a permanent [creator] cannot create things, whether gradually or all at once, there are no permanent things, whether external or internal.

8

Why [would] an efficacious [creator] be dependent? He would of course produce things all at once. A [creator] who depends on something else is neither eternal nor efficacious.

9

| gal te dngos na rtag min te |
| dngos rnams rtag tu skad cig phyir |
| gang phyir mi rtag dngos po la |
| byed pa po nyid bkag pa med |

10

| bdag sogs bral ba'i 'jig rten 'di |
| phung po khams dang skye mched dang |
| gzung dang 'dzin pa nyid dag gi |
| blo yis rnam par 'joms par 'gyur |

11

| phan par bzhed pa rnams kyis ni |
| gzugs dang tshor ba 'du shes dang |
| 'du byed rnam shes phung po lnga |
| de ltar nyan thos rnams la gsungs |

12

| rkang gnyis mchog gis rtag tu yang |
| gzugs ni dbu ba rdos dang 'dra |
| tshor ba chu yi chu bur 'dra |
| 'du shes smig rgyu dang mtshungs shing |

13

| 'du byed chu shing dang 'dra la |
| rnam shes sgyu ma lta bu zhes |
| phung po bstan pa 'di lta bu |
| byang chub sems dpa' rnams la gsungs |

14

| 'byung chen bzhi yi rang bzhin can |
| gzugs kyi phung por rab tu bshad |
| lhag ma gzugs med nyid du ni |
| med na mi 'byung phyir na 'grub |

9

If [he] were an entity he [would] not be permanent, for things are perpetually instantaneous (since [you] do not deny that impermanent things have a creator).

10

This [empirical] world, free from a self and the rest, is vanquished by the [Śrāvakas'] understanding of the skandhas, elements, sense-fields, and subject and object.

11

Thus the benevolent [Buddhas] have spoken to the Śrāvakas of the five skandhas: form, feeling, apprehension, karma-formations and consciousness.

12-13

But to the Bodhisattvas [the Buddha], the best among those who walk on two legs, has always taught this doctrine about the skandhas: "Form is like a mass of foam, feeling is like bubbles, apprehension is like a mirage, karma-formations are like the plantain, and consciousness is like an illusion."

14

The form skandha is declared to have the four great elements as its nature. The remaining [four skandhas] are inseparably established as immaterial.

15

| de dag rnams kyi mig gzugs sogs |
| khams rnams bshad pa de dag nyid |
| skye mched dag ni gzung ba dang |
| 'dzin par yang ni shes par bya |

16

| gzugs rdul med gzhan dbang po med |
| byed po'i dbang po shin tu med |
| skyod pa po dang skyed pa dag |
| yang dag bskyed par rigs ma yin |

17

| gzugs rdul dbang shes skyed min te |
| de ni dbang po las 'das yin |
| 'dus pa de rnams skyed byed na |
| tshogs pa de yang mi 'dod do |

18

| phyogs kyi dbye bas phye ba yis |
| rdul phran la yang dbye ba mthong |
| gang la cha shas kyis brtags pa |
| der ni rdul phran ji ltar 'thad |

19

| phyi rol don ni rnam gcig la |
| tha dad shes pa 'jug par 'gyur |
| yid 'ong gzugs ni gang yin pa |
| de nyid gzhan la gzhan du 'gyur |

20

| bud med gzugs ni gcig pu la |
| ro dang 'dod bya bza' ba la |
| kun rgyu chags can khyi rnams bzhin |
| rnam par rtog pa gsum yin no |

15

Among these eye, form, and so forth are classified as [the eighteen] elements. Again, as subject-object these are to be known as the [twelve] sense-fields.

16

Form is not the atom, nor is it the [organ] of sense. It is absolutely not the active sense [of consciousness]. [Thus] an instigator and a creator are not suited to producing [form].

17

The form atom does not produce sense consciousness, [because] it passes beyond the senses. If [empirical forms are supposed to] be created by an assemblage [of atoms], this accumulation is unacceptable.

18

If you analyze by spatial division, even the atom is seen to possess parts. That which is analyzed into parts – how can it logically be an atom?

19

Concerning one single external object divergent judgments may prevail. Precisely that form which is pleasant [to one person] may appear differently to others.

20

Regarding the same female body, an ascetic, a lover and a wild dog entertain three different notions: "A corpse!" "A mistress!" "A tasty morsel!"

21

| don mtshungs pa yis don byed pa |
| rmi lam gnod pa bzhin min nam |
| rmi lam sad pa'i gnas skabs la |
| don byed pa la khyad par med |

22

| gzung dang 'dzin pa'i ngo bo yis |
| rnam shes snang ba gang yin pa |
| rnam shes las ni tha dad par |
| phyi rol don ni 'ga' yang med |

23

| de phyir dngos po'i ngo bor ni |
| phyi don rnam pa kun tu med |
| rnam shes so sor snang ba 'di |
| gzugs kyi rnam par snang bar 'gyur |

24

| ji ltar skye bo sems rmongs pas |
| sgyu ma smig rgyu dri za yi |
| grong khyer la sogs mthong ba ltar |
| de bzhin gzugs sogs snang ba yin |

25

| bdag tu 'dzin pa bzlog pa'i phyir |
| phung po khams sogs bstan pa yin |
| sems tsam po la gnas nas ni |
| skal chen rnams kyis de yang spangs |

26

| rnams par shes par smra ba la |
| sna tshogs 'di ni sems su grub |
| rnam shes rang bzhin gang zhe na |
| da ni de nyid bshad bya ste |

21

Things are efficacious due to being *like* objects. Is it not like an offense while dreaming [i.e., nocturnal emission]? Once awakened from the dream the net result is the same.

22

As to the appearance of consciousness under the form of subject and object, [one must realize] that there exists no external object apart from consciousness.

23

In no way at all is there an external thing in the mode of an entity. This particular appearance of consciousness appears under the aspect of form.

24

The deluded see illusions, mirages, cities of gandharvas, and so forth. Form manifests in the same way.

25

The purpose of the [Buddha's] teachings about the skandhas, elements, and so forth is [merely] to dispel the belief in a self. By establishing [themselves] in pure consciousness the greatly blessed [Bodhisattvas] abandon that as well.

26

According to Vijñānavāda, this manifold [world] is established to be mere consciousness. What the nature of this consciousness might be we shall analyze now.

27

| 'di dag thams cad sems tsam zhes |
| thub pas bstan pa gang mdzad de |
| byis pa rnams kyi skrag pa ni |
| spang ba'i phyir yin de nyid min |

28

| kun brtags dang ni gzhan dbang dang |
| yongs su grub pa 'di nyid ni |
| stong nyid bdag nyid gcig pu yi |
| ngo bo sems la brtags pa yin |

29

| theg chen dga' ba'i bdag nyid la |
| chos la bdag med mnyam pa nyid |
| sems ni gdod nas ma skyes te |
| sangs rgyas kyis ni mdor bsdus gsungs |

30

| rnal 'byor spyod pa pa rnams kyis |
| rang gi sems kyi dbang byas te |
| gnas yongs gyur nas dag pa'i sems |
| so sor rang gi spyod yul brjod |

31

| 'das pa gang yin de ni med |
| ma 'ongs pa ni thob pa min |
| gnas phyir gnas ni yongs gyur pa |
| da lta ba la ga la yod|

32

| de ji ltar de ltar snang min |
| ji ltar snang de de ltar min |
| rnam shes bdag med ngo bo ste |
| rten gzhan rnam par shes pa med |

The Muni's teaching that "The entire [world] is mere mind" is intended to remove the fears of the simple-minded. It is not a [teaching] concerning reality.

[The three natures] – the imagined, the dependent, and the absolute – have only one nature of their own: śūnyatā. They are the imaginations of mind.

To [Bodhisattvas] who rejoice in the Mahāyāna the Buddhas present in brief the selflessness and equality of [all] phenomena [and the teaching] that mind is originally unborn.

The Yogācārins give predominance to mind in itself. [They] claim that mind purified by a transformation in position [becomes] the object of its own specific [knowledge].

[But mind] that is past does not exist, [while] that which is future is nowhere discovered. [And] how can the present [mind] shift from place [to] place?

[The ālayavijñāna] does not appear the way it is. As it appears – it is not like that. Consciousness essentially lacks substance; it has no other basis [than insubstantiality].

33

| ji ltar khab len dang nye bas |
| lcags ni myur du yongs su 'khor |
| de la sems ni yod min te |
| sems dang ldan bzhin snang bar 'gyur|

34

| de bzhin kun gzhi rnam shes ni |
| bden min bden pa bzhin du ni |
| gang tshe 'gro 'ong g·yo bar 'gyur |
| de tshe srid pa 'dzin par byed|

35

| ji ltar rgya mtsho dang ni shing |
| sems ni med kyang g·yo bar 'gyur |
| de bzhin kun gzhi rnam shes ni |
| lus brten nas ni g·yo ba yin |

36

| lus med na ni rnam par shes |
| yod pa min zhes yongs rtog na |
| de yi so so rang rig nyid |
| ci 'dra zhes kyang brjod par gyis |

37

| so so rang rig nyid brjod pas |
| de ni dngos po nyid du brjod |
| 'di de yin zhes brjod pa ni |
| nus min zhes kyang brjod pa yin |

38

| rang la de bzhin gzhan dag la |
| nges pa bskyed par bya ba'i phyir |
| rtag tu 'khrul pa med par ni |
| mkhas rnams rab tu 'jug pa yin |

33

When a lodestone is brought near, iron turns swiftly around;
[though] it possesses no mind, [it] appears to possess mind. In
just the same way,

34

The ālayavijñāna appears to be real though it is not. When it
moves to and fro it [seems to] retain the [three] existences.

35

Just as the ocean and trees move though they have no mind, the
ālayavijñāna is active [only] in dependence on a body.

36

Considering that without a body there is no consciousness, you
must also state what kind of specific knowledge of itself this
[consciousness] possesses!

37

By saying that a specific knowledge of itself [exists] one says it
is an entity. But one also says that it is not possible to say, "This
is it!"

38

To convince themselves as well as others, those who are
intelligent [should] always proceed without error!

39

| shes pas shes bya rtogs pa ste |
| shes bya med par shes pa med |
| de ltar na ni rig bya dang |
| rig byed med ces cis mi 'dod |

40

| sems ni ming tsam yin pa ste |
| ming las gzhan du 'ga' yang med |
| ming tsam du ni rnam rig blta |
| ming yang rang bzhin med pa yin |

41

| nang ngam de bzhin phyi rol lam |
| yang na gnyis ka'i bar dag tu |
| rgyal ba rnams kyis sems ma rnyed |
| de phyir sgyu ma'i rang bzhin sems |

42

| kha dog dbyibs kyi dbye ba 'am |
| gzung ba dang ni 'dzin pa 'am |
| skyes pa bud med ma ning sogs |
| ngo bo sems ni gnas pa min |

43

| mdor na sangs rgyas rnams kyis ni |
| gzigs par ma gyur gzigs mi 'gyur |
| rang bzhin med pa'i rang bzhin can |
| ji lta bur na gzigs par 'gyur |

44

| dngos po zhes bya rnam rtog yin |
| rnam rtog med pa stong pa yin |
| gang du rnam rtog snang gyur pa |
| der ni stong nyid ga la yod |

39

The knowable is known by a knower. Without the knowable no knowing [is possible]. So why not accept that subject and object do not exist [as such]?

40

Mind is but a name. It is nothing apart from [its] name. Consciousness must be regarded as but a name. The name too has no own-being.

41

The Jinas have never found mind to exist, either internally, externally, or else between the two. Therefore mind has an illusory nature.

42

Mind has no fixed forms such as various colors and shapes, subject and object, or male, female, and neuter.

43

In brief: Buddhas do not see [what cannot] be seen. How could they see what has lack of own-being as its own-being?

44

A 'thing' is a construct. Śūnyatā is absence of constructs. Where construds have appeared, how can there be śūnyatā?

45

| rtogs bya rtogs byed rnam pa'i sems |
| de bzhin gshegs rnams kyis ma gzigs |
| gang na rtogs bya rtogs byed yod |
| der ni byang chub yod ma yin |

46

| mtshan nyid med cing skye ba med |
| yod gyur ma yin ngag lam bral |
| mkha' dang byang chub sems dang ni |
| byang chub gnyis med mtshan nyid can |

47

| byang chub snying po la bzhugs pa'i |
| bdag nyid chen po'i sangs rgyas dang |
| brtse ldan kun gyis dus kun tu |
| stong pa mkha' dang mtshungs par mkhyen |

48

| de phyir chos rnams kun gyi gzhi |
| zhi zhing sgyu ma dang mtshungs par |
| gzhi med srid par 'jig byed pa'i |
| stong po nyid 'di rtag tu bsgom |

49

| skye med dang ni stong nyid dang |
| bdag med ces byar stong pa nyid |
| bdag nyid dman pa gang sgom pa |
| de de sgom par byed pa min |

50

| dge dang mi dge'i rnam rtog ni |
| rgyun chad pa yi mtshan nyid can |
| stong nyid sangs rgyas kyis gsungs gzhan |
| de dag stong pa nyid mi bzhed |

45

The Tathāgatas do not regard mind under the form of knowable and knower. Where knower and knowable prevail there is no enlightenment.

46

Space, bodhicitta, and enlightenment are without marks; without generation. They have no structure; they are beyond the path of words. Their 'mark' is non-duality.

47

The magnanimous Buddhas who reside in the heart of enlightenment and all the compassionate [Bodhisattvas] always know śūnyatā to be like space.

48

Therefore [Bodhisattvas] perpetually develop this śūnyatā, which is the basis of all phenomena; calm, illusory, baseless; the destroyer of existence.

49

Śūnyatā expresses non-origination, voidness, and lack of self. Those who practice it should not practice what is cultivated by the inferior.

50

Notions about positive and negative have the mark of disintegration. The Buddhas have spoken [of them in terms of] śūnyatā, [but] the others do not accept śūnyatā.

51

| sems la dmigs pa med pa ni |
| gnas pa nam mkha'i mtshann yid yin |
| de dag stong nyid sgom pa ni |
| nam mkha' sgom par bzhed pa yin |

52

| stong nyid seng ge'i sgra yis ni |
| smra ba thams cad skrag par mdzad |
| gang dang gang du de dag bzhugs |
| de dang der ni stong nyid 'gyur |

53

| gang gi rnam shes skad cig ma |
| de yi de ni rtag ma yin |
| sems ni mi rtag nyid yin na |
| stong pa nyid du ji ltar 'gal |

54

| mdor nasangs rgyas rnams kyis ni |
| sems ni mi rtag nyid bzhed na |
| de dag sems ni stong nyid du |
| ci'i phyir na bzhed mi 'gyur |

55

| thog ma nyid nas sems kyi ni |
| rang bzhin rtag tu med par 'gyur |
| dngos po rang bzhin gyis grub pa |
| rang bzhin med nyid brjod pa min |

56

| de skad brjod na sems kyi ni |
| bdag gi gnas pa spangs pa yin |
| rang gi rang bzhin las 'das pa |
| de ni chos rnams chos ma yin |

51

The abode of a mind that has no support has the mark of [empty] space. These [Bodhisattvas] maintain that development of śūnyatā is development of space.

52

All the dogmatists have been terrified by the lion's roar of śūnyatā. Wherever they may reside, śūnyatā lies in wait!

53

Whoever regards consciousness as momentary cannot accept it as permanent. If mind is impermanent, how does this contradict śūnyatā?

54

In brief: When the Buddhas accept mind as impermanent, why should they not accept mind as empty?

55

From the very beginning mind has no own-being. If things could be proved through own-being, [we would] not declare them to be without substance.

56

This statement results in abandoning mind as having substantial foundation. It is not the nature of things to transcend [their] own own-being!

57

| ji ltar bu ram mngar ba dang |
| me yi rang bzhin tsha ba bzhin |
| de bzhin chos rnams thams cad kyi |
| rang bzhin stong pa nyid du 'dod |

58

| stong nyid rang bzhin du brjod pas |
| gang zhig chad par smra ba min |
| des ni rtag pa nyid du yang |
| 'ga' zhig smras pa ma yin no |

59

| ma rig nas brtsams rga ba yi |
| mthar thug yan lag bcu gnyis kyi |
| brten nas byung ba'i bya ba ni |
| kho bo rmi lam sgyu 'drar 'dod |

60

| yan lag bcu gnyis 'khor lo 'di |
| srid pa'i lam du 'khor ba ste |
| de las gzhan du sems can gang |
| las 'bras spyod par 'dod pa med |

61

| ji ltar me long la brten nas |
| bzhin gyi dkyil 'khor snang gyur pa |
| de ni der 'pho ma yin zhing |
| de med par yang de yod min |

62

| de bzhin phung po nying mtshams sbyor |
| srid pa gzhan du skye ba dang |
| 'pho ba med par mkhas rnams kyis |
| rtag tu nges par bya ba yin |

57

As sweetness is the nature of sugar and hotness that of fire, so [we] maintain the nature of all things to be śūnyatā.

58

When one declares śūnyatā to be the nature [of all phenomena] one in no sense asserts that anything is destroyed or that something is eternal.

59

The activity of dependent co-origination with its twelve spokes starting with ignorance and ending with decay [we] maintain to be like a dream and an illusion.

60

This wheel with twelve spokes rolls along the road of life. Apart from this, no sentient being that partakes of the fruit of its deeds can be found.

61

Depending on a mirror the outline of a face appears: It has not moved into it but also does not exist without it.

62

Just so, the wise must always be convinced that the skandhas appear in a new existence [due to] recomposition, but do not migrate [as identical or different].

63

| mdor na stong pa'i chos rnams las |
| chos rnams stong pa skye bar 'gyur |
| byed po las 'bras longs spyod pa |
| kun rdzob tu ni rgyal bas bstan |

64

| ji ltar rnga yi sgra dang ni |
| de bzhin myu gu tshogs pas bskyed |
| phyi yi rten cing 'brel 'byung ba |
| rmi lam sgyu ma dang mtshungs 'dod |

65

| chos rnams rgyu las skyes pa ni |
| rnam yang 'gal bar mi 'gyur te |
| rgyu ni rgyu nyid kyis stong pas |
| de ni skye ba med par rtogs |

66

| chos rnams kyi ni skye ba med |
| stong nyid yin par rab tu bshad |
| mdor na phung po lnga rnams ni |
| chos kun zhes ni bshad pa yin |

67

| de nyid ji bzhin bshad pas na |
| kun rdzob rgyun ni 'chad mi 'gyur |
| kun rdzob las ni tha dad par |
| de nyid dmigs pa ma yin te |

68

| kun rdzob stong pa nyid du bshad |
| stong pa kho na kun rdzob yin |
| med na mi 'byung nges pa'i phyir |
| byas dang mi rtag ji bzhin no |

63

To sum up: Empty things are born from empty things. The Jina has taught that agent and deed, result and enjoyer are [all only] conventional.

64

Just as the totality [of their causes and conditions] create the sound of a drum or a sprout, [so we] maintain that external dependent co-origination is like a dream and an illusion.

65

It is not at all inconsistent that phenomena are born from causes. Since a cause is empty of cause, [we] understand it to be unoriginated.

66

That phenomena [are said] not to arise indicates that they are empty. Briefly, 'all phenomena' denotes the five skandhas.

67

When truth is [accepted] as has been explained, convention is not disrupted. The true is not an object separate from the conventional.

68

Convention is explained as śūnyatā; convention is simply śūnyatā. For [these two] do not occur without one another, just as created and impermanent [invariably concur].

69

| kun rdzob nyon mongs las las byung |
| las ni sems las byung ba yin |
| sems ni bag chags rnams kyis bsags |
| bag chags bral na bde ba ste |

70

| bde ba'i sems ni zhi ba nyid |
| sems zhi ba ni rmongs mi 'gyur |
| rmongs med de nyid rtogs pa ste |
| de nyid rtogs pas grol thob 'gyur |

71

| de bzhin nyid dang yang dag mtha' |
| mtshan ma med dang don dam nyid |
| byang chub sems mchog de nyid dang |
| stong nyid du yang bshad pa yin |

72

| gang dag stong nyid mi shes pa |
| de dag thar pa'i rten ma yin |
| 'gro drug srid pa'i btson rar ni |
| rmongs pa de dag 'khor bar 'gyur |

73

| de ltar stong pa nyid 'di ni |
| rnal 'byor pa yis bsgom byas na |
| gzhan gyi don la chags pa'i blo |
| 'byung bar 'gyur ba the tshom med |

74

| gang dag pha dang ma dang ni |
| gnyen bshes gyur pas bdag la sngon |
| phan pa byas par gyur pa yi |
| sems can de dag rnams la ni |
| byas pa bzo bar gyur par bya |

69

Convention is born from karma [due to the various] kleśas, and karma is created by mind. Mind is accumulated by the vāsanās. Happiness consists in being free from the vāsanās.

70

A happy mind is tranquil. A tranquil mind is not confused. To be unperplexed is to understand the truth. By understanding truth one obtains liberation.

71

It is also defined as reality, real limit, signless, ultimate meaning, the highest bodhicitta, and śūnyatā.

72

Those who do not know śūnyatā will have no share in liberation. Such deluded beings wander [among] the six destinies, imprisoned within existence.

73

When ascetics (yogācārin) have thus developed this śūnyatā, their minds will without doubt become devoted to the welfare of others, [as they think]:

74

"I should be grateful to those beings who in the past bestowed benefits upon me by being my parents or friends.

75

| srid pa'i btson rar sems can ni |
| nyon mongs me yis gdungs rnams la |
| bdag gis sdug bsngal byin pa ltar |
| de bzhin bde ba sbyin bar rigs |

76

| 'jig rten bde 'gro ngan 'gro yis |
| 'dod dang mi 'dod 'bras bu de |
| sems can rnams la phan pa dang |
| gnod pa las ni 'byung bar 'gyur |

77

| sems can brten pas sangs rgyas kyis |
| go 'phang bla med nyid 'gyur na |
| lha dang mi yi longs spyod gang |
| tshangs dang dbang po drag po dang |

78

| 'jig rten skyong bas brten de dag |
| sems can phan pa tsam zhig gis |
| ma drangs pa ni 'gro gsum 'dir |
| 'ga' yang med la mtshar ci yod |

79

| sems dmyal dud 'gro yi dwags su |
| sdug bsngal rnam pa du ma'i dngos |
| sems can rnams kyis myong ba gang |
| de ni sems can gnod las byung |

80

| bkres skom phan tshun bdeg pa dang |
| gzir ba yi ni sdug bsngal nyid |
| bzlog par dka' zhing zad med de |
| sems can gnod pa'i 'bras bu yin |

75

"As I have brought suffering to beings living in the prison of existence, who are scorched by the fire of the kleśas, it is fitting that I [now] afford them happiness."

76

The sweet and bitter fruit [that beings in] the world [obtain] in the form of a good or bad rebirth is the outcome of whether they hurt or benefit living beings.

77-78

If Buddhas attain the unsurpassed stage by [giving] living beings support, what is so strange if [those] not guided by the slightest concern for others receive none of the pleasures of gods and men that support the guardians of the world, Brahmā, Indra, and Rudra?

79

The different kinds of suffering that beings experience in the hell realms, as beasts, and as ghosts result from causing beings pain.

80

The inevitable and unceasing suffering of hunger, thirst, mutual slaughter, and torments result from causing pain.

81

| sangs rgyas byang chub sems nyid dang |
| bde 'gro dang ni ngan 'gro gang |
| sems can gang gi rnam smin kyang |
| ngo bo gnyis su shes par bya |

82

| dngos po kun gyis rten bya zhing |
| rang gi lus bzhin bsrung bar bya |
| sems can rnams la chags bral ba |
| dug bzhin 'bad pas spang bar bya |

83

| nyan thos rnams ni chags bral bas |
| byang chub dman pa thob min nam |
| sems can yongs su ma dor bas |
| rdzogs sangs rgyas kyi byang chub thob |

84

| de ltar phan dang mi phan pa'i |
| 'bras bu'byung bar dpyad pa na |
| de dag skad cig gcig kyang ni |
| rang don gnas zhin ji ltar gnas |

85

| snying rjes brtan pa'i rtsa ba can |
| byang sems myu gu las byung ba |
| gzhan don gcig 'bras byang chub ni |
| rgyal ba'i sras rnams sgom par byed |

86

| gang zhig bsgom pas brtan pa ni |
| gzhan gyi sdug bsngal gyis bred nas |
| bsam gtan bde ba dor nas kyang |
| mnar med pa yang 'jug par byed |

81

Know that beings are subject to two kinds of maturation: [that of] Buddhas [and] Bodhisattvas and that of good and bad rebirth.

82

Support [living beings] with your whole nature and protect them like your own body. Indifference toward beings must be avoided like poison!

83

Though the Śrāvakas obtain a lesser enlightenment thanks to indifference, the bodhi of the Perfect Buddhas is obtained by not abandoning living beings.

84

How can those who consider how the fruit of helpful and harmful deeds ripens persist in their selfishness for even a single moment?

85

The sons of the Buddha are active in developing enlightenment, which has steadfast compassion as its root, grows from the sprout of bodhicitta, and has the benefit of others as its sole fruit.

86

Those who are strengthened by meditational development find the suffering of others frightening. [In order to support others] they forsake even the pleasures of dhyāna; they even enter the Avīci hell!

87

| 'di ni ngo mtshar 'di bsngags 'os |
| 'di ni dam pa'i tshul lugs mchog |
| de dag rnams kyi rang lus dang |
| nor rnams byin pa ngo mtshar min |

88

| chos rnams stong pa 'di shes nas |
| las dang 'bras bu sten pa gang |
| de ni ngo mtshar bas ngo mtshar |
| rmad du 'byung bas rmad du 'byung |

89

| sems can bskyab pa'i bsam pa can |
| de dag srid pa'i 'dam skyes kyang |
| de byung nyid pas ma gos pa |
| chu yi padma'i 'dab ma bzhin |

90

| kun bzang la sogs rgyal ba'i sras |
| stong nyid ye shes me yis ni |
| nyon mongs bud shing bsregs mod kyi |
| de lta'ang snying rjes brlan 'gyur cing |

91

| snying rje'i dbang du gyur pa rnams |
| gshegs dang bltam dang rol pa dang |
| khab nas 'byung dang dka' ba spyod |
| byang chub che dang bdud sde 'joms |

92

| chos kyi 'khor lo skor ba dang |
| lha rnams kun gyis zhus pa dang |
| de bzhin du ni mya ngan las |
| 'das pa ston par mdzad pa yin |

87

They are wonderful; they are admirable; they are most extraordinarily excellent! Nothing is more amazing than those who sacrifice their person and riches!

88

Those who understand the śūnyatā of phenomena [but also] believe in [the law of] karma and its results are more wonderful than wonderful, more astonishing than astonishing!

89

Wishing to proteet living beings, they take rebirth in the mud of existence. Unsullied by its events, they are like a lotus [rooted] in the mire.

90

Though sons of the Buddha such as Samantabhadra have consumed the fuel of the kleśas through the cognitive fire of śūnyatā, the waters of compassion still flow within them!

91-92

Having come under the guiding power of compassion they display the descent [from Tuṣita], birth, merriments, renunciation, ascetic practices, great enlightenment, vietory over the hosts of Māra, turning of the Dharmacakra, the request of all the gods, and [the entry into] nirvana.

93

| tshangs dang dbang po khyab 'jug dang |
| drag sogs gzugs su sprul mdzad nas |
| 'gro ba 'dul ba'i sbyor ba yis |
| thugs rje'i rang bzhin can gar mdzad |

94

| srid pa'i lam la skyo rnams la |
| ngal so'i don du theg pa che |
| 'byung ba'i ye shes gnyis po yang |
| gsungs pa yin te don dam min |

95

| ji srid sangs rgyas kyis ma bskul |
| de srid ye shes lus dngos can |
| ting 'dzin myos pas rgyal 'gyur ba |
| nyan thos de dag gnas par 'gyur |

96

| bskul na sna tshogs gzugs kyis ni |
| sems can don la chags gyur cing |
| bsod nams ye shes tshogs bsags nas |
| sangs rgyas byang chub thob par 'gyur |

97

| gnyis kyi bag chags yod pa'i phyir |
| bag chags sa bon brjod pa yin |
| sa bon de dngos tshogs pa ni |
| srid pa'i myu gu skyed par byed |

98

| 'jig rten mgon rnams kyi bstan pa |
| sems can bsam dbang rjes 'gro ba |
| 'jig rten du ni thabs mang po |
| rnam pa mang po tha dad 'gyur |

93

Having emanated such forms as Brahmā, Indra, Viṣṇu, and Rudra, they present through their compassionate natures a performance suitable to beings in need of guidance.

94

Two [kinds] of knowledge arise [from] the Mahāyāna to give comfort and ease to those who journey in sorrow along life's path – so it is said. But [this] is not the ultimate meaning.

95

As long as they have not been admonished by the Buddhas, Śrāvakas [who are] in a bodily state of cognition remain in a swoon, intoxicated by samādhi.

96

But once admonished, they devote themselves to living beings in varied ways. Accumulating stores of merit and knowledge, they obtain the enlightenment of Buddhas.

97

As the potentiality of both [accumulations], the vāsanās are said to be the seed [of enlightenment]. That seed, [which is] the accumulation of things, produces the sprout of life.

98

The teachings of the protectors of the world accord with the [varying] resolve of living beings. The Buddhas employ a wealth of skillful means, which take many worldly forms.

99

| zab cing rgya che'i dbye ba dang |
| la lar gnyis ka'i mtshan nyid can |
| tha dad bstan pa yin yang ni |
| stong dang gnyis med tha dad min |

100

| gzungs rnams dang ni sa rnams dang |
| sangs rgyas pha rol phyin gang dag |
| de dag byang chub sems kyi char |
| kun mkhyen rnams kyis gsungs pa yin |

101

| lus ngag yid kyis rtag par ni |
| de ltar sems can don byed pa |
| stong nyid rtsod par smra rnams la |
| chad pa'i rtsod pa nyid yod min |

102

| 'khor ba mya ngan 'das pa la |
| bdag nyid che de mi gnas pa |
| de phyir sangs rgyas rnams kyis ni |
| mi gnas mya ngan 'das 'dir bshad |

103

| snying rje ro gcig bsod nams gyur |
| stong nyid ro ni mchog gyur pa |
| bdag dang gzhan don sgrub don du |
| gang 'thung de dag rgyal sras yin

104

| dngos po kun gyis de la 'dud |
| srid pa gsum na rtag mchod 'os |
| sangs rgyas gdung ni 'tshob don du |
| 'jig rten 'dren pa de dag bzhugs |

99

[Teachings may differ] in being either profound or vast; at times they are both. Though they sometimes may differ, they are invariably characterized by śūnyatā and non-duality.

100

Whatever the dhāraṇīs, stages, and pāramitās of the Buddhas, the omniscient [Tathāgatas] have stated that they form a part of bodhicitta.

101

Those who thus always benefit living beings through body, words, and mind advocate the claims of śūnyatā, not the contentions of annihilation.

102

The magnanimous [Bodhisattvas] do not abide in nirvana or saṃsāra. Therefore the Buddhas have spoken of this as "the non-abiding nirvana."

103

The unique elixir of compassion functions as merit, [but] the elixir of śūnyatā functions as the highest. Those who drink it for the sake of themselves and others are sons of the Buddha.

104

Salute these Bodhisattvas with your entire being! Always worthy of honor in the three worlds, guides of the world, they strive to represent the lineage of the Buddhas.

105

| byang chub sems 'di theg chen po |
| mchog ni yin par bshad pa ste |
| mnyam par gzhag pa'i 'bad pa yis |
| byang chub sems ni bskyed par gyis |

106

| rang dang gzhan don bsgrub don du |
| srid na thabs gzhan yod ma yin |
| byang chub sems ni ma gtogs pas |
| sangs rgyas kyis sngar thabs ma gzigs |

107

| byang chub sems bskyed tsam gyis ni |
| bsod nams phung po gang thob pa |
| gal te gzugs can yin na ni |
| nam mkha' gang ba las ni lhag |

108

| skyes bu gang zhig skad cig tsam |
| byang chub sems ni sgom byed pa |
| de yi bsod nams phung po ni |
| rgyal ba yis kyang bgrang mi spyod |

109

| nyon mongs med pa'i rin chen sems |
| 'di ni nor mchog gcig pu ste |
| nyon mongs bdud sogs chom rkun gyis |
| gnod min phrogs par bya ba min |

110

| ji ltar 'khor bar sangs rgyas dang |
| byang chub sems dpa'i smon lam ni |
| mi g·yo de ltar blo nyid ni |
| byang chub sems gzhol rnams kyis bya |

105

[In] Mahāyāna this bodhicitta is said to be the very best. So produce bodhicitta through firm and balanced efforts.

106

[In this] existence there is no other means for the realization of one's own and others' benefit. The Buddhas have until now seen no means apart from bodhicitta.

107

Simply by generating bodhicitta a mass of merit is collected. If it took form, it would more than fill the expanse of space!

108

If a person developed bodhicitta only for a moment, not even the Jinas could calculate the mass of his merit!

109

The one finest jewel is a precious mind free of kleśas. Robbers like the kleśas or Māra cannot steal or damage it.

110

Just as the high aspirations of Buddhas and Bodhisattvas in saṃsāra are unswerving, those who set their course on bodhicitta must make [firm their] resolve.

111

| ngo mtshar gyis kyang khyed cag gis |
| ji ltar bshad pa la 'bad kyis |
| de rjes kun bzang spyod pa ni |
| rang nyid kyis ni rtogs par 'gyur |

112

| rgyal mchog rnams kyis bstod pa'i byang chub sems ni bstod byas pa'i|
| bsod nams mtshungs med deng du bdag gis thob pa gang yin pa |
| de yis srid pa'i rgya mtsho dba' klong nang du nub pa yi |
| sems can rkang gnyis dbang pos bsten pa'i lam du 'gro bar shog |

111

No matter how amazing [all this seems], you must make efforts as explained. Thereafter you yourself will understand the course of Samantabhadra!

112

Through the incomparable merit I have now collected by praising the excellent bodhicitta praised by the excellent Jinas, may living beings submerged in the waves of life's ocean gain a foothold on the path followed by the leader of those who walk on two legs.

Notes on the Verses

1. I take bdag nyid dngos (or bdag nyid sku in A and C) as translating ātmabhāva, for which cf. May, op. cit., p. 278, n. 1017. In pāda b, A reads Śrī Vajradhara (dpal ldan rdo rje 'chang), whereas C speaks of rdo rje sems dpa'i sku (which it identifies with mahāmudrā, hence the epithet śrī, which may also be explained lha'i rigs phun sum tshogs pa dang ldan pa'i phyir ... etc. in accord with the Tantra [see 461a5-8]) without showing any sign of the plural. If B transmits the authentic reading I take this to indicate Bodhisattvas such as Samantabhadra, mentioned in BV 90, 111. For bhava see C 461b2: de la srid pa ni nye bar len gyi phung po lnga'i rang bzhin 'dod pa dang | gzugs dang gzugs med pa'i srid pa ste | 'byung zhing 'gyur ba'i phyir ro ||. Cf. MK XXVI, 8.

2. The genitive kyi (which C 462a2 also has) should be retained and construed with bzhed. It reflects *buddhānām ... mata or iṣṭa.

3. C 462a3 ff. lists the eight arthākāra of mahākaruṇā, explained in the Traité, p. 1707.

4-5. One cannot conceive ātman (skandhas) as eka or anya. MK XVIII; Schayer (1931), p. 90, n. 60.

6. A kāraka who is nitya is impossible, not only because there is no ātman (see above) but also because as a dharmin related to dharmas he would have to be anitya like them. See vv. 7-9. See also CS III, 34 with references in the note.

7-8. A creation all at once is against experience; a gradual one is incompatible with the notion of a creator's omnipotence (śakti/ sāmarthya). Cf. Siddhi, p. 30; Pramāṇavārttika l, 9 ff. This may be the earliest occurrence of this celebrated argument.

9. Being included among 'all things' a creator (C 463b7: dbang phyug la sogs pa) must also be anitya.

10. This refers to the Śrāvakas (BS 25-26 etc.). As in its canonical usage the term loko 'yam or ayam loka occasionally has a somewhat pejorative tone.

11. The Śrāvakas only endorse pudgalanairātmya, but by quoting a celebrated passage from their āgama (Saṁyutta III, p. 142; Sanskrit version in Prasannapadā, p. 41; cf. also Traité, p. 370) Nāgārjuna shows that even here we find evidence of the Buddha's teaching of dharmanairātmya. (Cf. CS I, 3 with references in the note.) See the discussion of Mahāyāna Buddhism in the Concluding Essay, below.

14. The following (vv. 14-24) constitutes a refutation of rūpa (i.e., upādāyarūpa [cf. Traité, p. 782] or bhautika), for which see CS I, 5 with references in the notes.

15. Cf. e.g. MK III-V.

16. A refutation of anu/paramāṇu; Traité, p. 725; Bhāvanākrama I, pp. 20-22; May (1959), p. 54, n. 15 (references). This is sūkṣmarūpa.

19. A refutation of sthūlarūpa. Cf. Traité, p. 733, which also cites the Sanskrit verse from the Sarvadarśanasaṁgraha. For further references consult Mimaki (1976), p. 309, n. 432. Similarly SS 60; Catuḥśataka VIII, 2; Saundarananda XIII, 52.

21. Though things can be efficacious, they are nevertheless śūnya. See the svavṛtti *ad* VV 22. For svapnopaghāta, see Viṁśatikā 4.

22. The following concludes that there is no bāhyārtha. Compare Mahāyānaviṁśikā 19: utpādo hi vikalpo 'yam artho bāhyo na vidyate ||. See also Laṅkāvatāra X, 154-155. But as we shall see the author takes great pains to show that the cittamātratā of the Laṅkāvatāra (see Suzuki's *Index,* p. 69) should be taken neyārtha; i.e. nairātmyāvatārataḥ.

24. Note that "dans les textes des Śrāvakas, on ne recontre jamais l'exemple de la ville de Gandharva" (Traité, p. 370); cf. also CS III, 5; RĀ II, 12-13 (cittamohana).

25. For the Sanskrit, see the Jñāśrīmitranibandhāvalī, p. 488 (with the variant reading citra).

26. The following (vv. 26-45) is a refutation of those who interpret cittamātratā, especially as presented in the Laṅkāvatāra, as nītārtha.

27. The Sanskrit can be found in the Subhāṣitasaṁgraha (ed. Bendall), p. 20; Jñānaśrīmitra, loc. cit. (with tattrāsa for uttrāsa)· Cf. Śikṣāsamuccaya, p. 263; Prasannapadā, p. 264, n. 2.

28. C 476b7: de la kun brtags ni gzung 'dzin te | phyi nang brtags pa tsam ni yin la rang bzhin med pa'i phyir ro | | gzhan dbang ni rtog pa'i rang bzhin te | rgyu rkyen gzhan dbang byas pa'i phyir ro | | yongs su grub pa ni gzung 'dzin gyi rnam par rtogs pa med pas so | | mi 'gyur bar yongs sh gnas pa'i phyir ro ||. For svabhāvatraya, see Laṅkāvatāra, pp. 127-133; CS III, 44; Siddhi, pp. 514-561. Nāgārjuna's position is that of Laṅkāvatāra II, 198.

29. This seems to allude to the verse quoted above as being from the 'Guhyasamāja'; now, however, it is a question of Bodhisattvas devoted to Mahāyāna! On the samatā of all dharmas, see e.g. Prasannapadā, p. 374.

30. For āśrayaparivṛtti (presented as here in the Laṅkāvatārasūtra) or āśrayaparivṛtti, see L. Schmithausen (1969), pp. 90-104. For the term svapratyātmagatigocara, see Suzuki's *Index*, p. 193.

31. Thus the author refutes this notion ekaprahāreṇa!

32. C 468b7: tshogs drug gi rnam par shes pa dang | nyon mongs pa can gyi yid ji ltar rnam pa dang dmigs pa dang snang ba de ltar kun gzhi ma yin te phyi rol gyi spyod yul la yongs su spyod mi nus pa'i phyir ro || des na ngo bo nyid bdag med rnam shes te don dam par rang bzhin med pa'i phyir ro ||.

33. For this comparison, see Laṅkāvatāra X, 14.

35. Ibid., X, 57-59.

37. One should not speak of that which cannot be spoken of. But here the author is not being quite fair; cf. MK XXII, 11.

38. Recalls Dhammapada XII, 2.

39. Cf. CS III, 50. Though B and A have rig bya / rig byed this surely refers to vedanāskandha (as v. 40 refers to saṁjñāskandha). Thus C469b7 is correct in having tshor bya / tshor ba. Cf. CS I, 6; ŚS 55.

40. Ibid., I, 7; III, 35 (with references in the notes).

41. Cf. ŚS 51.

42. citta (= manas = vijñāna) is – saṁvṛtitaḥ – arūpin. Thus it cannot be established by means of rūpa.

43. For the buddhacakṣus see CS II, 2: na ca nāma tvayā kiṁ cid dṛṣṭaṁ bauddhena cakṣuṣā |.

44. Cf. e.g. MK V, 7; XV, 4; May, op. cit., p. 92, n. 204. (śūnyatā = niḥsvabhāvatā = tattva = nirvikalpa, etc.)

45. Sanskrit in the Pañjikā, p. 406. Cf. CS II, 2: na boddhā na ca boddhavyam astīha paramārthataḥ |.

46. Sanskrit ibid., p. 421, with asaṁskṛtam in b (thus also C 471a8), which I have corrected to asaṁsthitam in accord with A (gnas pa med) and B (yod gyur ma yin). In pāda b, the Sanskrit may have read avākpatham (cf. CS IV, 1, etc.).

48. That is, śūnyatā destroys those dṛṣṭis which give rise to kleśa, karma, and punarbhava. Cf. MK XVIII, 5; YṢ 46-48; CS I, 23.

49. C 472a3 refers to MK XIII, 8. For bdag nyid dman pa, cf. alpa- buddhi (MK V, 8), mandamedhas (MK XXIV, 11); avipaścit (RĀ II, 19). The bdag nyid chen po is to the contrary: YṢ 50, 54.

50. All vikalpas are kṣaṇika; i.e., śūnya. Cf. v. 53. This is of course only saṁvṛtitaḥ; cf. RĀ I, 66-70.

52. The Sanskrit is found in the Caryāgīti (ed. Kværne), p. 246 with śatravaḥ, which I have emended in accord with A's rgol ba, B's smra ba and C's (dngos por) smra ba (472b5). For śūnyatā-siṁhanāda, see CS I, 22 and BS 101 with the accompanying note.

56. For this axiom see MK XV, 7-8.

57. Sanskrit in the Advayavajrasaṁgraha (ed. Śāstrī), p. 42.

58. The madhyamā pratipad avoids the extremes of uccheda and śāśvata. MK XV, 10; XVII, 21; CS III, 49.

59. As I have shown in *WZKS* XXVI (1982), these verses are quite closely related to the Pratītyasamutpādahṛdayakārikā. See also the Daśabhūmika (ed. Rahder), p. 50, which reduces avidyā, tṛṣṇā, and upādāna to kleśavartman, saṁskāra and bhava to karmavartman, and the remaining seven aṅgas to duḥkhavartman. As C observes (473b7), avidyā, saṁskāra, tṛṣṇā, upādāna, and bhava may also be regarded as hetu, whereas the remaining aṅgas are phala. Similarly in the small treatise Dharmadhātugarbhavivaraṇa ascribed to Nāgārjuna (see *IHQ*

XXXIII, pp. 246-249); cf. PK 4. See also Traité, pp. 349-351. For the final pādas of 63, see CS 1, 8; Saṁyutta II, pp. 75-76; Daśabhūmika, p. 49.

64. As the previous verses treated ādhyātmika-pratītyasamutpāda – saṁvṛtitaḥ, of course – this verse refers to bāhyapratītyasam-utpāda, presumably as treated in the Śālistambasūtra (quoted in the Pañjikā, pp. 577-579), though the bherīśabda (cf. Prasannapadā, p. 72) does not figure here.

65. In the saṁsāramaṇḍala any 'hetu' is also 'phala' and vice versa. Thus it is hetusvabhāvaśūnya. Cf. RĀ I, 36, 47.

66. Cf. RĀ IV, 86: anutpādo mahāyāne pareṣām śūnyatā kṣayaḥ |. For sarve dharmāḥ (= sarvam), see references in May, op. cit., p. 206, n. 689; see also YṢ 30.

67. Cf. MK XXIV, 8-10.

68. Here I understand saṁvṛti as sarve dharmāḥ (cf. Madhyamaka-hṛdayakārikā III, 13; also CS III, 44, with which compare Laṅkāvatāra II, 187). I take śūnyatā to equal pratītyasamutpāda (cf. MK XXIV, 18); i.e. pratītyasamutpanna (CS III, 44).

69. For the interpretation of this verse, see MK XVII, 26: karma kleśātmakam, and ibid., XVIII, 5: karmakleśā vikalpataḥ. For citta (= vikalpa), cf. Laṅkāvatāra III, 38: cittena cīyate karma. Again, citta itself is the outcome of previous karma (vāsanā) due to kleśa born from vikalpa (citta), etc. from time without beginning.

70. By thus destroying vikalpa (= citta, avidyā, etc.) by means of śūnyatā, the result is karmakleśakṣayān mokṣaḥ (MK XVIII, 5).

71. For other synonyms of the absolute, see CS I, 27; III, 37-41, 52; MK XVIII, 9; XXV, 3; ŚS 24.

72. Cf. YṢ 31.

53

73. What follows (vv. 74-104) is mainly devoted to an exposition
of the tathyasaṁvṛtibodhicitta (C 476a8) and only calls for a few
notes. In general we find here the same ideal of karuṇā as in the
Ratnāvalī, *Bodhisaṁbhāra[ka], and Śūnyatāsaptati.

77. On these gods, see RĀ I, 24; SL 69; Traité, pp. 137 ff.

81. C 477b8: sangs rgyas dang byang chub sems dpa' zag pa med
pa 'i dge ba'i rtsa ba'i las kyi rnam par smin pa 'i sems can no ||.
The vipāka specific to Buddhas and Bodhisattvas is the
kāyadvaya. Cf. BS 3 and references in the notes.

83. The Śrāvakas' pratisaṁkhyānirodha is inferior to the anuttarā
samyaksaṁbodhi of the Buddhas. Cf. Vimalakīrtinirdeśa, p. 422.
- Here, Lamotte has an import note on bodhimaṇḍam. It is the
locus of all virtues.

86. See BS 164 and references in the notes.

91. For pāda a cf. CS I, 1 with accompanying note. On the
Twelve Acts of a Buddha see e.g. CS II, 23;
Dvādaśakāranayastotra (Pek. ed. 2026); Bu ston I, p. 133 (the
verse cited by Bu ston as being from the Ratnāvalī is actually BV
91-92).

96. On puṇyajñānasaṁbhāra see RĀ III and the
Bodhisaṁbhāra[ka]. The ideal is to obtain two bodies.

97. See v. 81 above.

98. The Sanskrit is quoted in Sarvadarśanasaṁgraha (ed.
Abhyankar), p. 45 with cobha in 99b and bhinnā hi in 99c. Also
in Bhāmatī (ed. Sastri), p. 414 with kila in 98d. For the idea see
MK XVIII, 8; RĀ II, 35.

100 For dhāraṇī, see Traité, pp. 1854 ff. I have not traced the
Sūtra.

101. See v. 58 above.

102. Cf. BS 75 and references in the accompanying note, and G.M. Nagao in L.S. Kawamura (ed.), *The Bodhisattva Doctrine in Buddhism,* Waterloo, Ontario, 1981, pp. 61-79.

105. For similar bodhicittānuśaṁsā, see BS 57 and Bodhicaryāvatāra I.

110. In pāda a, A and C apparently read *saṁvaro (sdom pa) against B's *saṁsāre ('khor bar).

111. This refers to Samantabhadra's celebrated praṇtidhānas. For the Bhadracaryāpraṇidhāna (or Bhadracarīpraṇidhānarāja), see *Encyclopedia of Buddhism* II, pp. 632-638. I do not think that the commentary ascribed to Nāgārjuna (Pek. ed. 5512) is authentic. For a modem edition of the verses see J.P. Asmussen, *The Khotanese Bhadracaryādeśanā,* Copenhagen, 1961. See also SS 247b.

112. The final verse forms a pariṇāmanā. Cf. YṢ 60; CS III, 59; BS 165, etc. for other such dedications of merit.

Sources

A   Bodhicittavivaraṇa, tr. by Rab zhi chos kyi bshes gnyen et al. Pek. ed. 5470, Gi, fol. 221a-226b; Narthang ed. 3461, Gi, fol. 210b-215b.

B   Bodhicittavivaraṇa, tr. by Guṇākara and Rab zhi [chos kyi] bshes gnyen, revised by Kanakavarman and Nyi ma grags. Pek. ed. 2665, Gi, fol. 42b-48a; Narthang ed. 664, Gi, fol. 41b-46b.

C   Bodhicittavivaraṇaṭīkā, tr. by Smṛtijñānakīrti (the author). Pek. ed. 2694, Gi, fol. 454b-484b; Narthang ed. 693, Gi, fol. 449b-476b.

Variants

1a dngos B: sku AC
1b rnams B: 'chang A
6d spyod BC: dpyod A
(cf. Derge ed. 3868, Ya, fol. 344a4: dpyad)
8a ci de B : ci phyir A
10a 'di B :ni A
10cd A *pro*: gzung 'dzin blo yis 'joms par 'gyur B
12b dang 'dra A: 'dra snang B
14b bshad BA: gsal C
14d med na mi 'byung ... B : the tshom med par ... A
16 AC, *sed om.* B
17d tshogs pa de yang B: 'dus par yang ni A
19a ni rnam gcig la B : rnams gcig la yang A : ... rnam pa gcig dang | yang C
21b gnod pa bzhin min nam B: na ni rmis pa bzhin A : gnod sbyin don byed pa C (cf. Viṁśatikā 4)
23c snang ba 'di B: snang ba ni A : snang ba'i C
25b khams sogs BS: la sogs A
26c da B : 'dir A
28c gcig pu yi B: tshul gcig gi A
29c sems ni B: rang sems AC (*recte?*)

32b min AC : yin B
33d bzhin AC : zhing B
34c 'gro AC : sgra B
35 A valde differ
38a de bzhin B : nges bzhin A
40b 'ga' A : dga' B
41c kyis A : kyi B
42a kyi A :kyis B
46b yod gyur ma yin B : gnas pa med cing ACS
50a ni AC : gi B
51a dmigs pa BA : mtshan bya C; ni C(A) : yi B
51c ni B : 'di A
52b smra ba BC: rgol ba A
57a bu ram A : bur ram B
59a rga ba yi : rga shi'i (mtha') A: dga' ba yin B
63a las A: la B
68d byas : byas pa B
70d rtogs pas : rtogs pa B :rig pas A
74c yi: yis B (A quattuor pāda)
77a brten A: bsten B
80c zad med B : mi bzod AC
81a sems nyid B : sems dpa' A
83d kyi : kyis B : pa'i A
86a gang zhig BA : gang gis C
89c de byung nyid pas B: srid pa'i skyon gyis A(d)
90b A, sed om. B
94c ye shes (*jñāna-) B : theg pa (*yāna-) A(a)C
97c de dngos tshogs pa ni B: rjes mthar tshogs pa yis A(C)
98a kyi S : kyis B
101a rtag par : brtags par B : rtag tu A(b)C
102b de (cf. Tattvasārasaṁgraha 97a) : ste B : om. A
110b 'khor bar (*saṁsāra-) B : sdom pa (*saṁvara-) AC

12

phenapiṇḍopamaṁ rūpaṁ vedanā budbudopamā |
marīcisadṛśī saṁjñā saṁskārāḥ kadalīnibhāḥ ||

13

māyopamaṁ ca vijñānaṁ ... |

20

parivrāṭkāmukaśunām ekasyāṁ pramadātanau |
kuṇapaḥ kāminī bhakṣya iti tisro vikalpanāḥ ||

25

ātmagrahanivṛttyarthaṁ skandhadhātvādideśanā |
sāpi dvastā mahābhāgaiś cittamātravyavasthayā ||

27

cittamātram idaṁ sarvam iti yā deśanā muneḥ |
uttrāsaparihārārthaṁ bālānāṁ sā na tattvataḥ ||

45

na bodhyabodhakākāraṁ cittaṁ dṛṣṭaṁ tathāgataiḥ |
yatra boddhā ca bodhyaṁ ca tatra bodhir na vidyate ||

46

alakṣaṇam anutpādam asaṁsthitam avāṅmayam |
ākāśaṁ bodhicittaṁ ca bodhit advayalakṣaṇā ||

52

śūnyatāsiṁhanādena trasitāḥ sarvavādinaḥ |

57

guḍe madhuratā cāgner uṣṇatvaṁ prakṛtir yathā |
śūnyatā sarvadharmāṇāṁ tathā prakṛtir iṣyate ||

98

deśanā lokanāthānāṁ sattvāśayavaśānugāḥ |
bhidyante bahudhā loka upāyair bahubhiḥ punaḥ ||

99

gambhīrottānabhedena kva cid vobhayalakṣaṇā ||
bhinnāpi deśanābhinnā śūnyatādvayalakṣaṇā ||

BODHICITTAM **AND** *PHILOSOPHIA*

To have a head empty, like space, of all ideas, and a heart full of love – that is, very briefly, what Nāgārjuna's *Bodhi-citta-vivaraṇam* (*BCV*) is all about.

There is a red thread that runs through most of the works ascribed to the famous Nāgārjuna, some of which are edited in my book, *Master of Wisdom*. The same goes for his main work, the *Mūla-madhyama-kārikā Prajñā nāma*, of which I have for some time been preparing an English translation.

The main difficulty consists in tracing his sources and in deciding how he deals with these sources.

His main concern, or this red thread, is the proper understanding of the "profound Dharma", whereby he means *pratītyasamutpādas*, in Pāli: *paṭiccasamuppādo*.

The source of this notion is the *Dhamma-cakkappavattanasuttaṁ* (*DCP*) found at the very beginning of the *Mahāvagga* (*Mv*) (ed. H. Oldenberg, London 1879).

Students of Nāgārjuna must therefore begin with a careful reading of the *DCP*, above all in the earliest recension known to us, the one composed in Pāli. Nāgārjuna mainly used the recensions in Sanskrit. However, these recensions were made on the basis of the earlier one in Pāli.

The *DCP* is the fundamental scripture of any sort of Buddhism. Without it, there would, indeed, hardly be any such thing as "Buddhism" at all.

The *DCP* not only deals with *paṭiccasamuppādo*, but also with *majjhimā paṭipadā*, with the *ariyo aṭṭhaṅgiko maggo* identified with the right view, etc., with the four aspects of suffering, etc. etc. It is called the 'Unsurpassed Wheel of the Law', *anuttaraṁ dhammacakkam*. It is supposed to explain the meaning of the highest *bodhi*.

The *Dhammacakkam*, in Sanskrit *Dharmacakram*, is thus the most significant symbol of any kind of Buddhism, exactly as the Cross serves the same purpose in any kind of Christianity.

Strange as it may sound, the original meaning of the *Dharmacakram* is still anything but clear. Here we face a paradox: The deeper or original meaning of the fundamental symbol of a world religion is still quite obscure.

When one studies the *DCP* one should do something that modern scholars seem to have failed to do – one should count the number of words and syllables. The reason for this strange suggestion will be explained in a moment.

The next step, once this first step has been taken, is to see what Nāgārjuna has to say about the *DCP*. It will then be clear that Nāgārjuna deals with all the topics mentioned in the *DCP*. He, too, paid attention to each word and syllable mentioned in the *DCP*. And so must we. One must be a *gaṇite kṛtāvī* – an expert at counting, a "numerologist".

But to one's great surprise one must also notice that he superimposes or interpolates certain later ideas that are not to be found in the *DCP*. This is not what we would expect from an unbiased commentator. Now, what is the reason for this?

The *DCP* mentions *paṭiccasamuppādo* and *majjhimā paṭipadā*, but does not mention *śūnyatā* with one single word. Nor does it say that one has to go beyond "is" and "is not". Other, later sources do so. The "extremes" of which the *DCP* speaks, are of a different sort. Nāgārjuna, on the other hand, again and again, in almost all his works, insists that *śūnyatā* is the same as *paṭiccasamuppādo* (he uses the Sanskrit form, of course, *pratītyasamutpādas*, the nominative form).

The *DCP* mentions *paññā*, and understands it as instrumental in bringing about an understanding of *paṭiccasamuppādo*. As more or less synonyms of *paññā*, it lists *cakkhuṁ, ñāṇaṁ, vijjā* and *āloko* (*Mv* 1.6.23). Now and then we read *ārya-prajñā*, typically in the instrumental case.

In Nāgārjuna, however, *paññā* (Sanskrit: *prajñā*) has been replaced by *prajñā-pāramitā*, i.e. *prajñā* in a more perfected form. It suggests that the old term *prajñā* is not sufficient for a proper understanding of *paṭiccasamuppādo*. One of the synonyms of *paṭiccasamuppādo* is the compound *sa-hetu-dhammo*, or "causality". Already in the old *DCP*, the idea of *paññā* of causality is fundamental. The Lord is praised for being a *hetu-vādī*. He knows all about causality. A rather novel idea among Indians in those days.

In introducing *śūnyatā* and *prajñā-pāramitā* from various *sūtras* belonging to Mahāyāna, it cannot be denied that Nāgārjuna superimposes something that really, from a historical point of view, does not belong there at all. The way he again and again insists on their identity serves to confirm our suspicion of later interpretation. One employs more recent and familiar ideas in the hope of a better understanding of old ones. This can be risky.

He himself is not unaware of what he is doing. He must have felt a need to do so. We, as historians and philologists, must see if the reason for his strange step can be found. And why did other texts to which Nāgārjuna refers, take the same step? What was so obscure or problematic about the old *DCP* that later commentators felt the need to make such superimpositions? The distinction between two truths is yet another such superimposition. It is never mentioned explicitly in the *DCP* itself. Nor are things compared to dreams and illusions in the *DCP*. But Nāgārjuna himself repeatedly does so. (*BCV* 12-13, q.v. is no real exception to the rule.)

The problem has to do with the fact that the *dhammo gambhīro* – i.e. *paṭiccasamuppādo* – was said to be so extremely profound that it could only be understood by a very learned person, it was *paṇḍita-vedanīyo*, as the text says. We must pay attention to this compound.

Here is the original (*Mv* 1.5.2 , and later):

adhigato kho my āyaṁ dhammo gambhīro duddasso duranubodho santo paṇīto atakkāvacaro nipuṇo paṇḍitavedanīyo

– along with the translation of T.W. Rhys Davids & Hermann Oldenberg from 1881:

"I have penetrated this doctrine (*dhammo*) which is profound (*gambhīro*), difficult to perceive and to understand, which brings quietude of heart, which is exalted, which is unattainable by reasoning, abstruse, intelligible (only) to the wise (*paṇḍita-vedanīyo*)."

But what does that mean? What did this *paṇḍito* – "*bandido*" as the Mongolian pundits say – have to know in order to grasp the *dhammo gambhīro* properly? And what was it that common people could never be expected to know in order for them to grasp the *dhammo gambhīro*?

And who – a somewhat different issue – actually reported these words, that its discoverer spoke to himself? Did he say to others: This is what I said to myself?

The problem that eventually led to the formation of what we now refer to as Mahāyāna has part of its historical origin in the obscurity or ambiguity of the term *dhammo gambhīro*.

What then makes this *dhammo* so *gambhīro*? – we ask again.

Nāgārjuna often refers to this profundity, and claims that it has to do with *śūnyatā* and with the two truths. See his *Mūla-madhyamaka-kārikā*, XXIV, the main source, on the Āryan Truths.

But he is only partly right in claiming that the profundity has to do with *śūnyatā*. If the *dhammo gambhīro* had to do with *śūnyatā*, with two truths, with all things being like dreams, how come, then, that the *DCP* itself never says so in plain words? Instead, the *DCP* explains the *dhammo gambhīro* in terms of the *majjhimā paṭipadā*, and of causality, *sahetudhammo*, etc.

Here is a puzzle to be solved by the modern philologist!

To get on the track of the proper explanation of the profundity, one must start counting words and syllables. We shall soon see why this is the right path to follow!

So, if we count the number given by the 13 words above, beginning with *adhigato....*, we shall arrive at the number 6472/6471, which is almost exactly 4 x 1618, where 1618 is the number of the Golden Ratio. (The ambiguity is in the *my āyaṁ*, above.)

That each letter has exactly the same numerical value as in the Greek, or Ionian, alphabet, will come as a great surprise to Buddhist scholars, ancient as well as modern. But it is a fact that cannot be denied.

To be on the safe side, these 13 words are followed by these seven words:

ālayarāmā kho pana-ayaṁ pajā ālayaratā ālayasammuditā.

Counting each letter of these seven words, the grand total is 2043. Add 2043 to 6471 given above, and you get a grand total 8514.

But 8514 is exactly 2 x 2618 x 1.626. And 1.626 (for 1618+8 = 1626) is one of the values for the Golden Ratio. The Pythagoreans called it *Tetraktus* = 1626. In Sanskrit the Greek *tetra-ktus* becomes *catuṣ-koṭis*. This "golden soliloquy" obviously refers to *paṭiccasamuppādo*, the number of which is 1309. And 1309 is precisely one half of 2618 = 1000 + 1618.

This means that these terms and clauses were carefully fabricated in order to express the Golden Ratio. The man who did so may have been Indian, but he must also have been a Greek mathematician as well. Historians of Greek mathematics have shown that the properties of the Golden Ratio were first described in Ionia ca. 800 BC. They are, as I have pointed out elsewhere , behind the formation of the 24 letters of the Ionian alphabet.

I have counted the number of syllables and words of the *DCP* and related texts for many years, and the result was first presented to a learned audience at a conference in the Russian Academy of Sciences in Saint Petersburg, in November 2014 (yet to be published).

My conclusion was this: The *DCP* had been composed by Greek mathematicians. One must know Greek to make good sense of it all. It, the written text, works at two levels at the same time, one of narrative, one of numbers. The numbers are expressed in the numbers of letters and words.

I cannot here but give a few typical examples of how the *DCP* was composed on the basis of what we now refer to as the Golden Ratio. The authors were, in brief, Pythagoreans. The number of the Golden Ratio is, to repeat, 1.618.... It is, naturally, also reflected in 2618 (=1000+1618), in 1118 (= 618+500), in 1236 (= 618 + 618), etc. In addition, it is reflected in other combinations of the last two digits. The number 1, from where all starts, is 0.618... x 1.618....

If one takes the trouble to make a list of all proper names and technical terms found in the *DCP*, one will be able to confirm that they have, all of them, been fabricated on the basis of the digits 1618, or 1681 (same digits), etc.

And what about the ***Bodhi-citta-vivaraṇam***, the number of which is 1711? Solution: 1711 is what you get when you multiply 1601.8... x 1.0681....The same goes for the *sa-hetu-dhammo* (above) = 1061, where 1061 is thus really 1061.8.

Another very early text is the *Dhammapadam* (= 212), and it contains ca. 423 verses. The reader can easily discover the number of the Golden Ratio behind the names, for all names refer to numbers. This early text was composed with the Golden Ratio in mind.

When we here speak of the Golden Ratio, this, to be sure again, not only refers to the four digits 1.618... in that order, but likewise to the very same four digits in the order given for the solution of 1711.

This then is the hidden meaning of the term *paṇḍitavedanīyo* – only a Greek mathematician can understand the deeper meaning of the *dhammo gambhīro*.

This explanation should be sufficient to grasp the "psychological" reason for Bhagavā being reluctant to expound the *dhammo gambhīro* to common people. It would be as difficult as to explain something in Mongolian to people who do not know the Mongolian language at all!

But at the same time, the language of numbers would serve as a sort of universal language. So there was hope!

Scholars like Pythagoras, Plato, Euclid would have been fascinated – as opposed to most other people. But Mahāyāna is, as the word itself indicates, not for the few, but for the many.

The ancient Pythagoreans made a sharp distinction between insiders, who were called mathematicians, and outsiders, who were merely expected to listen to the insiders. They were called "listeners". That is the meaning of *śrāvakas*. Nāgārjuna often refers to those "who just listen". (So does Jesus!)

The *DCP* cannot possibly have been composed before the time of Alexander the Great. The common view that "the Buddha" lived one, two, or three centuries before Alexander is not only to be rejected for lack of solid and reliable external evidence, but even more so by the mathematical Greek nature of the *DCP* itself.

In the form given, it cannot possibly have been created by any Indian *Buddho Bhagavā* living some obscure place in India centuries before the coming of the Ionians. How in the world could he, all on his own, make great mathematical discoveries, that it took Ionian scholars such a long time finally to make? And even if *Buddho Bhagavā* be defined as a Greek mathematician, he must have lived *after* Alexander the Great. The *DCP* itself contains obvious myths, and is, as a whole, mathematical, rather than historical literature. The Greeks, the Macedonians, told many myths about their gods, and this was certainly one of them – the only one that eventually made it into the flag of modern India. The intention was, briefly, to reform the Indian "barbarians" by way of Greek *paideia*, which included what we later refer to as the quadrivium. It is fundamental to the Pythagoreans.

And it is exactly here that we have the reason for Nāgārjuna feeling the need to pour new wine into the old bottle of the *DCP*. He too, was familiar with Greek science (*Master of Wisdom*, p. 310, n. 79).

Clearly, gematria of this sort, cannot possibly be expected to have any popular appeal at all. It would not attract converts, but rather scare them away.

So the new idea was introduced: All things are empty. You therefore just need to have faith in the Buddhas and Bodhisattvas, and then you will be saved! The Buddhas love you and you must love all other living beings. Your faith will save you! This is the simple message of Mahāyāna. Common people can never understand what *Tathāgata(s)* saw and understood. But they should have faith in his profound mathematical genius. It cannot be calculated! Thus faith replaces scientific insight.

I may here be permitted to insert the remark that the New Testament in Greek provides a perfect parallel to this. The Greek text was composed by mathematicians, who carefully counted words and syllables. This is a fact. A minority of NT theologians are aware of this undeniable fact. But they seldom inform the common Christian believer about this. Exactly as in Mahāyāna, there is an appeal to faith, not to scientific or mathematical insight.

There are, to be sure, a few ancient reports to the effect that early Christians were mathematicians who studied Euclid along with the holy scriptures. Still, the best proof is to be found in the very text of the Greek NT itself. Any theologian can check that out for himself! Ironically, numerology was condemned in Nicæa AD 325!

At this point we see Nāgārjuna showing two faces, as it were. A numerical analysis of his *Mūla-madhyamaka-kārikā Prajñā nāma* shows that this book was composed on the basis of the Golden Ratio. He never says so in plain words; thus the fact has escaped ancient and modern scholars to this very day.

The number of the title *Mūla-madhyamaka-kārikā Prajñā nāma* is 471+118+154+243+92 = 1079. Multiply then 1079 x 1.5, and you get ca. 1618 – the digits of the Golden Ratio. Geometrically, this means that the 1618 circle contains a 1078.666 "fish". The round number is 1079.

The number of Prajñā is 243. Multiply 243 x 4.44, giving you 1079. But 4.44 is ca. 1.681 x 1.615 x 1.618. The 27 chapters of his book consists of exactly 14,368 syllables (in Sanskrit only, of course), which is 888 x 1.618 x 10. (The number 3, above, is

1 +1 + 1, and 1 = 0.618 x 1.618.) It, too, was composed on the basis of the Golden Ratio. His own name, with the Greek article, was *ho Nāgārjunas* = 888 = 2 x 444 = 4 x *bodhi-maṇḍam* (= 222). So was his *Śūnyatā-saptati* = 963 + 892 = 1855, which is ca. 3 x 5 x 1.236... (= 0.618 + 0.618) x 10 x 10. In the text itself, the author often inserts words from the passage on the *dhammo gambhīro*, to be sure. These facts only a *bandido* will want to be aware of.

Behind the various Buddhist terms translated as "wisdom", we find various surnames of the Greek goddess of Wisdom, Athênê, known as Pronoia, Pronaia, Sophia, etc. She, too, was mother and virgin at the same time. She became the female object of worship in Mahâyâna. When Mahâyâna worshpis Wisdom, it worships Athênê under various new names. In Christianity, Athênê again appears as mother and virgin at the same time. And here again she becomes the mother of a great king and son of God, etc. No wonder, then, that Maria or Mariam is often identified with Sophia, or Wisdom. Amaria was one of the surnames of Athênê. In a few sources she was identified with Maia, otherwise mother of Hermës. To Buddhists she is here known as Mâyâ.
But back to our author!

To him *satya-dvaya-vibhāgas* is of fundamental importance. Its number is 512 + 924 + 618 = 2054. Here, *vibhāgas* = 618 refers to the Golden Ratio. Multiply 618 by 2 x 1.6618..., giving you 2054, or the like. Hence the natural distinction between insiders and outsiders, a typical Pythagorean distinction, as said. Buddhism began with the introduction or discovery of *paṭiccasamuppādo*. Count each letter as if it were Greek, and you get the grand total 1309, or ½ of 2618 = 1618 + 1000 (major and minor)..
Take then the clause where *Buddho Bhagavā* admits to himself: *adhigato kho*..., as quoted above. The number of the letters was 4 x 1618.

Following the *DCP*, I have repeated myself a few times.

Or take *Tathāgato*, never explained properly by scholars, ancient or modern; the number is 686, i.e. 161.8... x 1.618... x 1.618... x 1.618 = 686. (Remember that names always are round numbers!)

The anonymous authors of at least some of the recensions of the *DCP* in Sanskrit were fully aware of these numerical mysteries. The proof is provided by a numerical analysis that any student can conduct for himself. Some of them have been critically edited by Franklin Edgerton in his *Buddhist Sanskrit Reader*, New Haven 1953.

The term *paṭiccasamuppādo* = 1309 provides a fine example of this. The Sanskrit is *pratītyasamutpādas* (always nominative forms to start with!). The number is 2030. How do these two figures compare? – As follows: *paṭiccasamuppādo* is 432 + 877 = 1309. Here, 877 divided by 432 = 2.030. But 2030 is the number of the Sanskrit compound! So here you have a wonderful example of the meaning of "dependent origination" – the one depends on the other in terms of numbers (digits). Language and numbers depend on one another. Numbers begin to speak.

Now, what occurs when 2030 is divided by 1309? We then get the ratio 1.55. But 155 shows the digits of *dhammo* = 4+1+40+40+70 = 155! - And 155 = 1.6 x 6 x 1.615 (the 21:13 ratio, a "Fibonacci" number, valid for the Golden Ratio; 5:3, 8:5, 13:8 and 21:13, giving an average of 1.62676).

You can go on and on like this, and you will invariably come to the conclusion that the *DCP* is the work of a great mathematical genius fully familiar with Greek theology.

The Pythagorean idea was that the names of the gods refer to numbers. The gods are but names, but numbers are as real as can be. Hence the Buddhist idea about all things being mere names. It means that they are all numbers.

Historically, the properties of the Golden Ratio are to be found geometrically in the pentagram, the secret symbol of the Greek Pythagoreans. Behind each Buddhist term, the number of the name of one or more Greek gods will be found. Thus, early Buddhism does not merely represent Greek geometry. It also represents Greek theology.

The various philosophical ideas found on the surface of the *DCP* can easily be traced back to Greek sources. That includes the idea of knowing yourself, of suffering, of rebirth, of a middle path between extremes leading to liberation, etc. etc.

Even emptiness, the Greek *to kenon*, has a clear Pythagorean source.

As said, the study of Mahāyāna must begin with the study of the *DCP*. But, likewise, the study of the *DCP* must begin with the study of Greek philosophy, above all that of the Pythagoreans. Pythagorean philosophy includes geometry and theology, as known.

For details, a modern student will want to consult the relevant Greek sources for him- or for herself. There are, surely, many fine modern works on Greek philosophy (W.K.C. Guthrie, *A History of Greek Philosophy*, Vol.1, Cambridge 1963. etc.), but still the serious student must go to the primary Greek sources. Autopsy of original sources is essential, now as before.

Plato did not want students ignorant of (Greek) geometry to enter his Academy. The very same piece of good advice is now offered to serious students of Indian Buddhism!

Let us now briefly see how *Bodhi-citta-vivaraṇam* fits into this picture!

The *DCP* speaks of *bodhi-*, it speaks of *citta(m)*, and it uses the verb *vivareyya* (*Mv* 1.7.10). On this basis the title *Bodhi-citta-vivaraṇam* was fabricated. One must be a *bandido* to know!

In the *BCV* the author then, on this basis, makes a distinction between two kinds of *bodhi-cittam-* as others had done before him, but all on the basis of the *DCP*.

One has to do with practical life, motivated by compassion, another with theoretical life, personal freedom. One for the head, another for the heart.

The distinction has roots far back in Greek philosophy. Virtue, *aretē*, has two aspects, a practical and a theoretical. The distinction between *actio vitae* and *cognitio veri* is fundamental to almost any kind of classical philosophy. The Indians originally got it from the Greeks, and it can only have happened after Alexander the Great. The distinction was familiar to all educated Greeks centuries before the time of Alexander, whose tutor was, we must not forget, no other than Aristotle. Nāgārjuna takes up the two aspects of wisdom again in the first chapter of the *Ratnāvalī*, q.v. It is constantly repeated in later Buddhist and non-Buddhist sources, even among the so-called Jainas.

In Mahāyāna, then, emphasis is on emptiness and on faith, and on compassion, or, if you will, "love". Rituals such as confessions of one's sins, also play a considerable role. The promise is given that all of us can eventually become Buddhas. Here, there is room for the worship of a saviour of all mankind. He descended from heaven to teach us all the path to immortality. So, his loving kindness deserves our gratitude and worship, surely. The idea that this great man and god thus sacrificed himself (on a cross or elsewhere) is thus the fundamental myth common both to Mahāyāna and Christianity; its copy, Jesus, is just one in a long line of Buddhas.

This idea was completely foreign to the anonymous Greek mathematicians or Indian disciples, who composed the *DCP*. (Indians gone Greek, or Greeks gone Indian – who can decide?) The Greek ideal is intellectual, mathematical, scientific.

Several of Nāgārjuna's other works demonstrate that he was perfectly familiar with "Hīnayāna". He was, in fact, a follower of both, depending on circumstances. Here, one may speak of "a leap of faith". That there are different teachings for different people is a typical idea of Mahāyāna. It is expressed thus in one of the 112 verses of the *BCV* that has managed to survive in Sanskrit (v. 98):

deśanā lokanāthānāṁ sattvāśayavaśānugāḥ |
bhidyante bahudhā loka upāyair bahubhiḥ punaḥ ||

Different kinds of Buddhism for different kinds of people – that is what this highly problematic adage says. There are probably naïve souls who will find it offensive to speak of Mahāyāna Jesuitism – but that is what it is. The masses ask for *panem et circenses*, and Mahāyāna willingly offers the miracles and beliefs the superstitious masses crave for.

Now, what kind of reader did Nāgārjuna have in mind when he composed his *BCV*?

We do not know for sure. But the very fact that he wrote in Sanskrit reduces his readership to a minority. He probably wrote it to learned monks and householders.

How many copies were made? We have no idea.

Translations into Chinese, Tibetan (and later on, Mongolian) were made. The original Sanskrit has been lost, only fragments have survived, cited here and there in later commentaries or anthologies. We must always keep the distinction between erudite insiders and "religious" outsiders in mind.

The situation has hardly changed, when we consider modern Christianity – a sort of crypto-Mahāyāna. Popes and priests appeal to faith rather than to reason. It has become a somewhat risky business for the minority that appeals to reason and science (cf. e.g. Richard Dawkins, *The God Delusion*, Boston & New York 2006). Popes and priests claim that there is a world beyond reason, a world of faith in its own right.

They are wrong, but understand very well that such deceit is required to fool the masses, for is it not true that *mundus vult decipi*?

Buddhism and Christianity – *Jinaputras*

Mahāyāna and New Testament Christianity have much in common. No wonder, for if I am not quite mistaken, the NT can and should, historically speaking, be seen as a sort of Mahāyāna propaganda. The *Lotus Sūtra* provides a blueprint. Jesus is a new Buddha, merely one of many. Śāri-Putras now appears under a new name: Simōn Petros, etc. etc. The names of the four evangelists can easily be traced back to Buddhist sources. The same goes for the authors of the "epistles" found in the NT. Pythagoreans and Mahāyāna Buddhists often composed such "epistles".

It is the old story of the son of God who descended from above to teach the way to immortality. The Greek Saviour, *sōtēr*, becomes the Indian *trātā*, also meaning Saviour. (Typically, the number *of sōtēr* is 1408, the number of *trātā* is 704, one half of 1408).

The narrative is much the same, with a strong appeal to faith that is supported by a great number of parables and miracles. Little or nothing of all this has anything to do with what we would consider to be true or actual history. One must be very naïve to think that these "holy texts" report "what actually happened".

Still, priests make a good living by representing mere stories as if they were real history. The history of the Church, as has been said, is by and large a history of deception. Naturally, Christian scholars cannot be expected to look upon the history of their own church in that light.

Interestingly, Nāgārjuna himself compares the Buddha to an illusion or a dream – which is more than many modern scholars would dare or even dream of doing. But he is writing for insiders.

As far as I am aware, no modern theologian would dare to compare Jesus Christ to an illusion or a dream. Peter called him a phantasm – rightly so.

A few days ago – on December 17th, 2014 – the Pope declared in public that not only Jesus Christ but also Adam and Eve were real, historical persons.

Such and similar irresponsible public statements intended to appeal to the ignorant masses – are typical of Mahāyāna propaganda. There is no sharp distinction between stories and tales on the one hand, facts and history on the other. I would even go a step further and say, quite frankly: There is no respect for truth!

And what about the Dalai Lama? He has written and spoken widely not just about Buddhism but also about Christianity.

He knows what a Buddhist has to know about *Śāri-Putras*, just as his colleague in Rome knows all there is to know about *Simōn Petros*.

It is Cicero who tells the story about two augurs who upon meeting have a hard time suppressing their laughter.

Any competent scholar of Buddhism and Christianity must, when he compares the two, come to the conclusion that *Simōn Petros* is no other than *Śāri-Putras* in disguise. The myth of the successor to the founder has its source in *Suttanipātaṁ*, vv. 556-567, *q.v.*

But where are the scholars who have the courage to step forward and inform the public accordingly? What a great shame!

A few days ago, world media reported that the Dalai Lama was in Rome but that the Pope did not wish to see him.

Oh? Such a meeting could have been very interesting, had the Dalai Lama known the history of his own religion.

How so?

The current Pope, Francis, is said to be No. 266 in an awesome lineage beginning with Simōn Petros, first bishop of Rome. Vatican officials even have the audacity of pointing to his grave!

Had I been Dalai Lama, I would have raised this issue, forgetting all about "emptiness" and "love" etc. etc. Mahāyāna, we are told, advocates the ideal of a Bodhisattva, a human being whose head is as full of emptiness and whose heart is almost as full of "love". ("Love" here normally refers to love of myth, as opposed to love of truth.)

The terminology is extremely important!

In several verses of the *BCV* the author employs the term *Jina-putras* as a synonym of the more common Bodhisattva(s).

A *Jinaputras* is the great human hero of Mahāyānism – and of Christianity!

First, to be sure, in the *DCP*, *Buddho Bhagavā* refers to himself as a *Jino* (Pāli), in Sanskrit: *Jinas*. In Mahāyāna, his followers, become his "son(s)", *putras*. And so we have the *Jinaputras* (nominative sing.).

One of the main *Jinaputras*, even the first of them all, is no other than the famous *Śāri-Putras*.

And here we have the historical link that with one stroke undermines the authority of the Roman papacy: In the New Testament, *Matthew 16:17*, Jesus addresses *Simōn Petros* as *Bar-Iōna(s)*. Here, the Aramaic *Bar-*, son, translates the meaning of the Sanskrit *putras*, and the *-Iōnas* renders the sound of the Sanskrit *Jinas*. The context is the same in both sources; it has to do with the secret of the Lord.

In other words: The Buddhist *Śāri-Putras* as *Jina-putras* is transformed into the first Christian pope: *Simōn Petros* as *Bar-Iōnas*. The direct Buddhist source I have identified many years ago (see Michael Lockwood, *Buddhism's Relation to Christianity*, Chennai 2010, p. 263) is the *Saddharmapuṇḍarīkasūtram*, to which there are numerous allusions etc. in the NT as a whole.

The conclusion, that I, had I been the Dalai Lama, would have taken up for friendly "inter-faith" discussion with Pope Francis, is inevitable: The authority of the Roman papacy is founded on an old Buddhist myth. More diplomatically: Francis is not No. 266 – only No. 265 – in a house of cards!

Here, then, to be quite sure, is the simple historical truth that in itself will undermine the credibility of Christianity:

Śāri-Putras Jinaputras has been resurrected as Simōn Petros Bar-Iōnas.

So, a *Jinaputras* is the great human ideal of Mahāyāna and, *mutatis mutandis*, of NT Christianity. Indeed, does not Jesus say that all his disciples can become "sons of god" (*Matthew 5:9*), Sanskrit *devaputras*, yet another synonym of *Jinaputras*.

So, the idea is that first you are a *Jinaputras*. You thereby hope and strive to become a *Jinas*. But what does that mean?

And it gets even better. In *Peter 5:1*, Peter, the alleged author, defines himself as a *sum-presbuteros*. He, then, is one *presbuteros* among several such "Christians". But without a shadow of doubt, the Greek *presbuteros* here translates the Buddhist *thero* (Pāli), Sanskrit: *sthaviras*. They are synonyms. Not only so: *Sāri-putto* (Pāli) = 1462 = *presbuteros* = 1462.

The *BCV* employs the term we are looking for, twice. When a *Jinaputras* has ended his long career, he becomes a *Jinas*, or *Buddhas*, and thereby enters, or sits down in what is called a *Bodhi-maṇḍam*.

Now *Bodhi-maṇḍam* is not an easy word compound.

In the *DCP* it is said that this *bodhi* takes place at the root of the Bodhi-tree, *bodhi-rukkha-mūle* (there is an allusion to this - *mūle* in the title of Nāgārjuna's <u>*Mūla*</u>*-madhyamaka-kārikā Prajñā nāma*).

The corresponding Sanskrit is, however, in most cases, and in the *BCV*, *bodhi-maṇḍam*, which could be rendered as "temple of bodhi". (The Tibetan rendering, of *maṇḍam*, *snying po*, heart, is misleading.) The Japanese *Dōjō*, to be sure, understands it as a place or platform of *bodhi*.

In the art of Gandhāra we see examples of a Buddha sitting in what is presumably such a *bodhi-maṇḍam*. Understood in more secular terms this would seem to indicate that he has now become a great king dwelling there on his royal throne, sometimes even surrounded by soldiers – Macedonian soldiers or guardians! This, again, immediately reminds us of the motif so common on Hellenistic coins – the enthroned father Zeus.

This understanding is in harmony with the idea, found in some of Nāgārjuna's other works, that a *Jinas* is the father of all the *Jinaputras*.

These Hellenistic images of father Zeus enthroned have, as far as I can judge, a common root, namely Phidias' statue of Zeus at Olympia, one of the Seven Wonders of the ancient world. All educated Greeks, and tourists from afar to Olympia, would have been aware of this.

The Buddha seated in a *bodhimaṇḍam* is, I suggest, the Buddhist version of Zeus enthroned in the temple, and depicted on coins. Later on, as known, Jesus, was *pantokratōr*, and was portrayed in the likeness of his father, Zeus.

The father of Jesus was also "enthroned", and so is Jesus himself! These are but tales, stories, that have nothing to do with history. And yet this is merely the "worldy" side of the coin. Thus, the number of *bodhi-maṇḍam* is 86 + 136 = 222.

And 222 = 141.4 x 1.57. And 222 is 2 x 111, where 111 is 1.618 x 68.6. And 686, as pointed out above, is the number of *Tathāgato* (Pāli), or of *ārya-satyāni* (Sanskrit).

To make sense of *bodhi-maṇḍam*, you must know Greek.

Zeus, (the) God, is the great geometrician; and, as such, he knows all about the basic ratios, including the square root of two, and the number of Π (1.57 x 2 = 3.14).

The term *bodhi-maṇḍam* is thus a geometrical term. To dwell in a *bodhi-maṇḍam* means to be an expert mathematician – which is the ultimate ideal of a *Jinaputras*.

I mentioned Peter. Among the 27 books of the New Testament, we also find two letters or epistles ascribed to Peter. Interestingly, NT scholars do not agree about the authenticity of these two letters, originally composed in the Greek language.

Most remarkably, the author of the first letter ascribed to Peter – I mentioned that above – describes himself as a *presbuteros* along with other "elders". The Greek is a precise synonym of *thero* in Pāli, and *sthaviras* in Sanskrit.

The number of *presbuteros* is 1462, which is also the number of *Sāri-putto*.

In Buddhism there are many later works ascribed to *Śāri-putras*. So it was only to be expected that this practice would be continued in the New Testament which, as said, is Mahāyāna propaganda.

The two letters of Peter therefore serve as a fine introduction to what Mahāyāna assimilated to Judaism may look like.

The Mahāyāna authors of the NT had a great sense of humour. We now know who *Bar-Iōnas* really was. And now we – as opposed to traditional NT theologians – also know why Jesus called *Jinaputras* a "scandal"!

It remains a scandal to this very day, to pious Christians and to pious Buddhists. The founder of the Church was a mythical Buddhist!

The *DCP* made it clear that the *dhammo gambhīro* was an extremely profound matter. It was *paṇḍita-vedanīyo*, only to be known and understood by profound mathematicians. But it was also, as the text explicitly states *paramaṁ sukhaṁ* – the highest form of happiness.

All people want to be happy, we are told. Should you desire to become a *Buddho Bhagavā*, should you wish to be *vimuttisukhapaṭisaṁvedī*, you, too, will have to learn to calculate according to the Golden Ratio, the most profound principle of eternal nature, as the Pythagoreans believed.

If this is too much, you may still remain a "*sutavā ariya-sāvako*", (first in *Mahāvagga* 1.6.46), the number of which is 2118, i.e. 1618 + 500. Here, 500 is 22.36 x 22.36; and 22.36 is 16.18 + 6.18.

So the Golden Ratio is always there.

This finally brings us to a good historical definition of 'Buddhism' and 'Buddhist'. A true Buddhist is a student of the Golden Ratio, which also implies the other fundamental ratios, beginning with the square root of 2, or 1.414, etc.

All this is is what the Pythagoreans would call the holy Philosophy, *hē hagia philosophia* = 8+15+1391 =1414.

To follow the *majjhimā paṭipadā* – itself an expression of the middle proportion – leads you to *upasamo, abhiññā, sambodhi* and *nibbānaṁ* = 792 + 115 + 327 + 157 = 1391.

The source of Buddhism is Pythagorean. Buddhism came from the Pythagoreans.

The idea of *śūnyatā* as *anutpādas* is typical of the *Prajñā-pāramitā*. The *DCP* also spoke of *prajñā*, almost as a synonym of *bodhi*; it is by means of *prajñā* that one understands *pratītyasamutpādas*.

Without *prajñā* there is no such thing as Buddhism. The Greek synonym, and original, is *sophia*. Quite precisely, *sophia* is the ability to count correctly. Love of wisdom is the love of maths, of numbers, of geometry.

The number of *prajñā* is 243. Multiply by 2 x 1.6081, and you get ca. 781 – the number of the original Greek *sophia*. Or multiply ca. 243x2.43 (same digits) and you get *majjhimā paṭipadā*, whereas in Greek is the sum of Pythagorean *monas* and *dekas* (361+230 = 591) 591 is also Athênê parthenos. So, *śūnyatā* is something to be understood by *prajñā* in a more perfect form, *pāramitā*.The notion of all dharmas (numbers, things, ratios) being empty, can be traced back to Pythagorean sources. The Sanskrit *śūnya-tā* is a perfect translation of the Greek *to kenon*. (Greek *to* becomes Sanskrit *tā*!)

The Greek sources of the Pythagorean *to kenon* are conveniently edited in the fine collection of text by H. Ritter & L. Preller, *Historia philosophiae graecae*, Gotha 1913, p. 64.

Their idea is as follows. To begin with there is an *infinitum*, an *apeiron*. That corresponds exactly to the Buddhist *anantam*, said of *nirvāṇam*. It is from the Infinite that Time, Air and the Void somehow, through space, *ouranos*, enters this world, the *kosmos*.

In the *BCV*, the void, or emptiness, is compared to space.The term to *asuntheton* is also Pythagorean (*op. cit.*, p. 65). The Sanskrit *asaṁskṛtam* is a literal translation. In the *BCV* it is clear to the author that *śūnyatā* and *pratītyasamutpādas* are much the same thing. But, in what is, therefore, perhaps his later works, *Mūla-madhyamaka-kārikā* and *Śūnyatāsaptati*, he stresses the point that *madhyamā pratipad(ā)* has the very same meaning.

The meaning of this statement is only obvious once we consider it in terms of geometry. When, say, the diameter is 282.8, then the circumference of the circle is 888. The two depend on one another; you cannot take one away without removing the other. The phrase *madhyamā pratipad(ā)* thus has the meaning of mean proportion. Something, say A, may be long in relation to, say B, but short in relation to, say C. It makes no sense to speak of A, B, or C as long or short taken in themselves. The mean proportion is a proportion, or logos, that links the two (or more) together. As such, in itself, it is not empty. To the extent that it depends, it is. Keeping this simple fact in mind, it is obvious that *pratītyasamutpādas*, *śūnyatā* and *madhyamā pratipad(ā)* have the same meaning, that they are *eka-artha(m)*.

Again, the *DCP* had nothing to say about two kinds of *satyaṁ*. One had to do with words, the other was beyond words. Here, too, we are dealing with geometry. It is only when we use words properly, that is when we count the words and syllables, that we recognize the correct numerical ratios.All that has here been said or written, makes sense (I hope), but it also makes numbers (of that I am sure). The early *DCP* based its discourse on this Pythagorean distinction.

I invited readers – not mere listeners – to count. So let us summarize:

The *DCP* spoke about *bodhi*, a synonym of *prajñā*. It spoke about *cittaṁ*, and about a *cittaṁ* that was *vimuttaṁ*, released, i.e. by seeing the basic mathematical ratios, concentrated in the Golden Ratio.

Buddho Bhagavā, a geometrical figure, also had a practical *cittaṁ*, one that motivated him to rescue ignorant beings by way of *dhammadesanā*. So, here we have the double *bodhicittaṁ*. In the *DCP*, he is praised for having revealed what is hidden, *paṭicchannaṁ vivareyya* (*Mv* 1.7.10). So, we have the title *Bodhicitta-vivaraṇam*. Then there was the deeper or more perfect form of *prajñā*, the *prajñā-pāramitā*. It was concerned with *śūnyatā*. To some extent this was implicit, but not explicit in the *DCP*.

The ideal is still the same – one wants to enjoy personally the happiness of freedom, to be *vimutti-sukha-paṭi-saṁvedī*.

The highest happiness is peace, as when a difficult problem has been solved. But all is not peace. There are two worlds. The ideal is then to escape from the world of impermanence and suffering. There is a distinction between *niccaṁ* = 141, and *aniccaṁ* = 142.

Add the two, and you get the diameter of the 888.62 or 889 circle of *Buddho Bhagavā*, etc. You must know the mysteries of the Pythagoreans to achieve this aim. Going back to the beginning of the *DCP*:

Bhagavā discovered the law of *paṭiccasamuppādo* (= 1309 = 1/2 of 2618) at the root of the tree of *bodhi*; in *bodhirukkhamūle* = 1102 = 160.81 x 2.618 x 2.618.

Later on, we have the synonym: *bodhimaṇḍam* = 222; but 222 is 1.414 x 1/2 of Π. Words refer to numbers, and the *prajñā* of numbers, makes you free and happy.

The name of his own philosophy is *śūnyatā-vādas* = 1570, or 10 x 157 = 5 x 314 (the digits of Phi) ca. 6 x 261.8.

Nāgārjuna is undeniably a philosopher of the Golden Ratio.

Theravādo Means Philosophia

The earliest form of Buddhism known to us understood itself as *Theravādo* Its main doctrine was that of *paṭiccasamuppādo* and of the *majjhimā paṭipadā*. All other doctrines are derived from these two notions. Can these fundamental notions be traced further back, perhaps? We are here dealing with what the Pythagoreans called *philo-sophia*. In their view, all things were numbers or had numbers.This rule, of course, also applies to the very term *philo-sophia*, said to have been coined by Pythagoras himself.

The number of *philosophia* is 610+781=1391.

When you divide the figure 1391 by 781, you get the ratio 1.781. Looking at 781 for *sophia*, and 1.781 as the ratio linking *sophia* up with *philo-sophia*, you immediately see a "harmony of digits". The three digits are, to be quite sure: 7-8-1.

The number of *Theravādo* is 9+5+100+1+400+2+4+70 = 591.The number of *majjhimā paṭipadā* = 40+1+10+10+11+40+2+80+1+300+10+80+1+4+2 = 591. So the two are in a numerical sense the same, or equivalent – for 591 is undeniably 591.

This is the typical Pythagorean way of thinking. It may seem strange to us, but our feelings about this are utterly irrelevant. Historical facts are there to be respected by us.

In the *DCP* it is explicitly written that the *majjhimā paṭipadā* leads to or is in harmony with (*saṁvattati*) with these four "virtues": *upasamo, abhiññā, sambodhi,* and *nibbānaṁ*. Their numbers are: 792+115+327+157= 1391.

Speaking in two languages as these people did, we may say that *majjhimā paṭipadā* leads to or is in harmony with *philo-sophia*. Moreover, the *DCP* explicitly states that *majjhimā paṭipadā* is *cakkhu-karaṇī* and *ñāṇa-karaṇī*, the numbers of which are, respectively, 643 and 285, adding up to 928.

Here there is a hidden meaning that only is revealed to a Greek geometrician: If you draw 591 as a cross, then you have the two diameters in the 927.87 circle. It's thus quite true that 591 forms an eye (for you to see), and enables you to know. For knowing is a matter of seeing. When you double up 927.87, you arrive at 1855.74. But what does this figure have to do with *philo-sophia*?

To answer that question, you must go back to the Greek Pythagoreans, who often depicted *philo-sophia* as an equilateral triangle inscribed in a circle, the circumference of which is 1681.1626.

The 1391 equilateral triangle consists of three straight lines, each of which is 463.666....

You can now represent four of these as a regular square = 1854.666.... The circle in which such a square is inscribed will then be 2058.6799.

Divide, first, the 1854.666 square by 2, and you get 927.333..., or 928 – the sum of 643+285, exactly as just explained above.

The relationship between *Theravādo* & Greek *Philosophia* has thus been accounted for in terms of geometry.

It can also be accounted for in terms of numerology, to the very same effect.

Start with 591; multiply by 1.5, giving you 886.5. Multiply this by 1/2 of Π, which is 157, the number of the mysterious *nibbānaṁ,* and then you again land on ca. 1391.005.In this way it may safely be claimed that the earliest and most original form of Buddhism, calling itself *Theravādo,* represents what the Pythagoreans chose to call *Philo-sophia.* – The other technical term was, as said *paṭiccasamuppādo* = 1309. How are 1309 and 1391 related?

Answer: Multiply 1309 by 1.0626, and you get 1391. If you read 1309 as 1309.1, the digits are the same.

In 1.0626 you immediately see the digits that were seen in the 1681.1626 circle containing the inscribed equilateral triangle of the 1391 *philosophia.*

Finally, it may be recalled that *Theravādo* had an expression for "a good Buddhist", namely *sutavā ariya- sāvako* = 1303 + 122 + 693 = 2118. But 2118 is 5 x 423.6, and 423.6 is 1.618 x 2.618.

The figure 2118 also links up with 188, for ca. 188 x 6 x 1.88 is ca. 2118. (Quite precisely, 18.8016 x 18.8016 = 353.5, or 1/4 of 1414.)

And when *hē hagia* = 23 was added to 1391, we landed on 1414 – the digits of the square root of 2.

This figure is, of course, as Pythagorean as can be; and this is where the most comprehensive term of them all comes in:

In the final analysis, Dhammacakkam = 188 is thus derived from the square root of one quarter of 1414.

Likewise, *Dharmacakram* = 328 is derived from 1414 thus. First divide 1414 by 3/4, giving you 1060.5. Divide then 1060.5

by 1.618, giving you 656 = 2 x 328. In Pāli, we have *sambodhi* = 327 (from 1/2 of the Golden Ratio of 3/4 of the initial 1414).

Buddhism is thus derived directly from the theorem of Pythagoras. The Greeks had a technical term for this: The Hellenic Canon, or *kanōn ho hellēnikos* = 1414. Another Greek phrase is *autos ho logos* (= 971+70+373) , i.e. logos itself.

Linking up with the above, we have 1414 = *hē hagia philosophia*.

Theravādo is a "Presentation" (*pavattanaṁ/pravartanam*) of this, designed for insiders and listeners alike. Once this is given, so is the square root of five, and thereby also the number of the Golden Ratio. A good Buddhist is, in other words, a "man of the Golden Ratio", i.e. a good Pythagorean. The reader will now be able to make further amazing discoveries: It was said that 591 leads to 1391 = *upasamo* + *abhiññā* + *sambodhi* + *nibbānaṁ*. Now, take *sambodhi* = 327, or almost 328.

The 591 *majjhimā paṭipadā* was specified as *ariyo aṭṭhaṅgiko maggo* = 191+755+117 = 1063. And it was clear that it, as such, i.e. as 1063 was much the same (*saṁvattati*) as *sambodhi*. This is true, and here is the simple proof: ca. 1063 + ca. 327/328 = 1391.

In the Sanskrit tradition, *sambodhi* becomes the famous *Dharma-cakram* = 146 + 182 = 328. That brings us back to the 2059 circle mentioned above.
Its radius was 327/328.

2059 is the number of the *Saddharma-puṇḍarīka-sūtram*. And 2059 is also the number of two of its main characters, namely *Śāri-Putras* = 1393 , and *Maitreyas* = 667; adding up to ca. 2060.

Inscribed in this circle, we found the ca. 1855 square, which was 2 x ca. 927.4..., and so we are safely back at 1391, for 1391 x 4/3 is, indeed, ca. 1855.

When you then multiply 328 x 2 x 1.618, you get ca. 1061, the number of *sa-hetu-dhammo*, a synonym of *paṭiccasamuppādo*.

When you then multiply 1061/1062 by 1.309 (the digits of *paṭiccasamuppādo*), you again land on ca. 1391.

It is, in conclusion, perfectly correct to claim that Theravādo is all about Greek philosophia – the love of numbers.

For reasons given above, common Buddhists and Christians will not be happy with this conclusion, no matter how true to historical fact it may be. Also, erudite Buddhist and Christian scholars will not be happy with this conclusion. They must keep silent not to scare their ignorant supporters away.

The title of this essay is *Bodhicittam* = 748 and *Philosophia* = ca. 1391. The two terms are rationally related as follows:

748 x 1.15 (the digits of *abhiññā*) x 1.618 = 1391.8036, or 1391.

So to speak of *Bodhicittam* is yet another way of presenting Greek *Philosophia*.

Dhammacakkam & Dharmacakram

I mentioned that these terms were in some respects still rather obscure. In some respects, however, the meaning can now be made quite clear. Naturally, the terms somehow refer to the well-known wheel. But how so?

First the number of *Dhammacakkaṁ* (Pāli) is 188; and if one lets 188 be the number of the diameter of a circle, the circumference of the circle will be ca. 591, and 591 is the number of *majjhimā paṭipadā*.

Then there is *Dharmacakram* (Sanskrit), which is 328. If one, in the very same way, lets 328 be the radius of the circle, then the circumference is ca. 2059, the number of *Saddharmapuṇḍarīkasūtram*, and, at the same time, the sum of *Śāri-Putras* + *Maitreyas*, two main figures in that very text. This is the meaning of "the second turning" (misunderstood by later Buddhist tradition).

This means that the circumference of the wheel is determined by the name-number of the diameter or radius.

Yet another possibility is to let 328 appear as a three-pointed star inscribed in a circle. The diameter of the circle is thus 218.666; and the circumference accordingly ca. 686.61333.... But 686 is evidently the number of *Tathāgato* (Pāli), and of *ārya-satyāni* in Sanskrit.

Going back to the 591 circle of *majjhimā paṭipadā* (Pāli), we are told that this event took place in Benares, *Bārāṇasiyaṁ*, the number of which is 418. But 418 is the very number of the circle inscribed in the ca. 532 square inscribed in the 591 circle. It will be easy for the reader to discover that all other locations etc. given in the *DCP* are derived in the same way on a purely geometrical basis. – From this it follows that the events took place in geometry, not in geography.

The narrative is thus clearly a myth, as opposed to the mathematical facts revealed by the numbers. In this sense, one can safely claim that all these stories are like dreams and illusions.

Another example: If 188 for *dhammacakkam* be the circumference of the circle, then the inscribed equilateral triangle will be ca. 155; but 155 is the number of *dhammo*.

And again: If 328 be the circle, then the inscribed equilateral triangle will be ca. 271.5. Here, 272 is the number of *Dharmapadam*, whereas 271 is the number of *Jinas* (Sanskrit).

Divide then 188 by 1.6081 (the digits of the Golden Ratio), and you land on ca. 117, which is the number of *maggo* (Pāli).
Let then ca. 328 be the circle; here, the inscribed three-pointed star is ca. 157, which is the number of *nibbānaṁ* (Pāli).

The square in such a ca. 328 circle is ca. 295.5. , and three such squares thus add up to 887/888. But 887 is the number of the highest ideal: *Mahāparinirvāṇam* (Sanskrit). The number of *paññā* (Pāli) is 183, the octagon in the 188 circle of *Dhammacakkaṁ*.

Let then 188 be the "fish" in the 282 circle, where 282 is *saccaṁ* (Pāli). Add the two, giving you 470; multiply by 1.414..., giving you 665; but 665 is the number of *ārya-satyam* (Sanskrit).

If 328 be taken as the round number of ca. 328.93 (which is allowed), then the circle is ca. 889 – the number of *Buddho Bhagavā*, the highest human ideal.

Let 188 be the equilateral triangle inscribed in the 227.2168 circle. The two squares inscribed in this circle add up to 409, the very number of *Bhagavā* (Pāli).

And now that *Bhagavā* has been found, how do you find *Buddho* (Pāli) = 480? Start, as always with 188. Multiply by 1.626 (Golden Ratio), giving you 305.688, which is the cross in the 480 circle of *Buddho* (Pāli). Combine *Buddho Bhagavā* = 889, which is ca. *Theravādo* x 1.5. And as *Theravādo* = *majjhimā paṭipadā* was derived from the ca. 188 diameter, so is *Buddho Bhagavā* = *Siddhāttho* (=889) = *Mahāsamano Gotamo* (=405 + 484).

Moreover, *bodhimaṇḍam* was 222. This is also derived from the 328 circle: The hexagon in a 328.656... circle is ca. 314.... Divide ca. 314 by the square root of 2, and you get ca. 222 for *bodhimaṇḍam*.

1309 is the number of *paṭiccasamuppādo*, and that is what you get, when you multiply 188 x 2.12 (digits of *dhammapadaṁ*) x 3.28... (digits of *dharmacakram*); thus you get 1309, which is 1/2 of 2618 (= 1000 + 1618).

And again: Multiply 1.414 x 1.414 x 1.414 x 1.414 = ca. 5.656.... Multiply ca. 188 for *Dhammacakkam* by ca. 5.656, and you get exactly 1063; but 1063 is the very number of the phrase *ariyo aṭṭhaṅgiko maggo* = 191+755+117 = 1063.

What these examples (easily to be multiplied) show us, is that the numbers ca. 188 and ca. 328 can be applied in various ways, arithmetically or geometrically, so as to bring forth new numbers that correspond to those key concepts that serve to define "Buddhism".

All the figures given may, naturally, be associated with wheels or circles. This must be the context in which the meaning of the term *pravartanam* or *pavattanaṁ* be properly defined.

The meaning is, as we have just seen, that the numbers 188 and 328 have the power or potential to produce all the fundamental concepts of "Buddhism". The term must thus mean "power of production" So, "Buddhism" was produced from the *Dhammacakkaṁ* (Pāli) or the *Dharmacakram* (Sanskrit).

Buddhism, we can now sum up, started with a simple drawing of a ca. 888 circle. The figure 888 can only apply to an abstract circle, whereas the corresponding physical wheel may thus have a circumference of ca. 889, and on the inside, e.g. 887.

The diameter in such as circle is then represented by *saccaṁ* (Pāli = 282), or by *sammā* (Pāli = 283). The rim of a wheel is then somewhere between ca. 885.48 and 888.62. Five diameters add up to ca. 1414 – the digits of the square root of two. Thus Buddhism began with the "fingerprint of Pythagoras".

Once 1414 was given so was 1618, 1732, 1626, etc. It is all summarized in the *Dhammacakkam* or *Dharmacakram*.

And so *pravartanam* (Sanskrit) or *pavattanaṁ* (Pāli) is a technical geometrical term that refers to the productive power of the numbers of *Dhammacakkam* and *Dharmacakram*, as well as to its "presentation". The term *anuttaraṁ dhammacakkam* is 1381, i.e. ca 1.236 x 111.8. For the Greeks, 1381 equals 600 + 781 = *su* + *sophia* = *You are Wisdom*.

THE LORD HAS TWO BODIES

In some of his other works, Nāgārjuna deals with the ideal of *bodhi* from a somewhat different perspective, that is of great comparative interest to us here. He refers to the Mahāyāna doctrine of two bodies. A Buddha, he claims, is a great Man who has two bodies, one is made up of good karma, the other is spiritual, and consists in knowledge of universal Emptiness. There is a clear distinction between a *rūpakāyaḥ* and a *dharma-kāyaḥ*. It is described in details in the third chapter of the *Ratnāvalī*, of which there is an English translation by Jeffrey Hopkins, *The Precious Garland*, New York 1975.

I invite students of Buddhism and Christianity to read this chapter carefully along with my own translation from the Chinese of *Pú ti zî liáng lùn* (Taishô No. 1660). It will be found in my *Master of Wisdom*.

Once this has been done, one should turn to the NT, to *1 Corinthians 15*, which is largely based on Buddhist sources. Here, "Paulos (=781=sophia)" makes a clear distinction between the two: "If there is a physical body, there is also a spiritual body" (v. 44). The physical body is perishable, the spiritual body is imperishable, he says. Theologians have always, with "Paul" himself (v. 51), considered this doctrine of two such different bodies of the Lord a "mystery", for which no rational explanation could be given.

This "mystery", however, becomes less mysterious once we go *ad fontes*, i.e. once we see that "Paul" here follows Mahāyāna, without, of course admitting so in plain words. If one fails to consult the original Buddhist source, the Pauline doctrine of two bodies will, indeed, remain a mystery to all Christians. That this strange doctrine is also somewhat of a mystery even to Buddhist scholars is a problem in its own right. The Buddhists probably wished to assimilate themselves to ancient Vedic ideas about a great Man. This assimilation to Vedic tradition must have taken place at a very early date, giving later commentators the impossible task of making good sense of it. Buddhists still believe in this Great Man, with his 32 major and 80 minor marks. Note that 80 / 32 = 2.5. But who ever saw him with his own eyes? Paul left the Buddhist phantasm as a "mystery".

A critical edition, with notes and the Tibetan as well as Sanskrit fragments of the *BCV*, was first published in my book (doctoral dissertation): *Nagarjuniana: Studies in the Writings and Philosophy of Nāgārjuna*, Copenhagen 1982. It has often been reprinted in India. – A revised American edition appeared under the title *Master of Wisdom*, 1986. It, too, has often been reprinted.

For a fine introduction to the Golden Ratio, see Mario Livio, *The Golden Ratio: The Story of Phi, the World's Most Astonishing Number*, 2002. (The author, however, ignores the Christian and Buddhist sources.)

For Buddhist sources of the New Testament, see my: *Geheimnisse um Jesus Christus*. Süderbrarup, 2005 (and later). The Danish version was immediately banned. The numbers always came before the names.

The author is grateful to Prof. Michael Lockwood who read a first draft and offered valuable suggestions. In his view, Buddhism may well have been made by Indian scholars residing in Alexandria.

The coins of *Athênê*

Athênê Promakhos is often found on the ancient Greek coins of king Menander. The *anutarram dhammacakkam* was 1381, and when we write ê Athênê Nikê ê Promakhos, we get 8 + 76 + 88 + 8 + 1161 = 1341. When we add an *ekei* = 40, meaning "here", we land on 1381. The founders of Buddhism had the same goddess in mind as those who erected and admired the temples and statues of *Athênê* on the Athens Acropolis. The coins, the temples and the statues are in complete harmony with the symbolism of the wheel on the modern Indian flag. The Wheel is her Aigis.

The formation of *Prajñā-Pāramita*

The number is 243 + 535 = 778. Let, again 188 be the diameter in the 591.32 circle. Add the two, and you get 778.32. So it has the same source as *Thera-vādo* (591) with the 188 diameter of *Dharmacakkam* etc. For the Greeks, 243 is *Athênê Erganê* (78+167). The number 778 says *eimi Parthenos Korē* = I am the Virgin Maiden. 779 says you are (*su ei*) *Athēnē Nikē* (600 +15 + 76 + 88). So, She remains the secret source of any sort of Buddhism.